# Stress without Distress

HANS SELYE, M.D.

A SIGNET BOOK

NEW AMERICAN LIBRARY

TIMES MIRROR

Portions of this book have appeared in *House & Garden,
Intellectual Digest* and *Physician's World.*

The section "Work and Leisure" in Chapter 2 is based on
Dr. Selye's article "On Stress and the Executive," which has
appeared in *Executive Health Report.*

This is an authorized reprint of a hardcover edition published
by J. B. Lippincott Company.

Library of Congress Catalog Card Number: 74-1314

# STRESS IS NOT SOMETHING TO BE AVOIDED

The only way to avoid stress would be to do nothing at all. Virtually all human activity involves stress—from a game of backgammon to a passionate embrace. But this can be defined as the stress of pleasure, challenge, fulfillment. What we all want is the right kind of stress for the right length of time—at a level that is best for us. Excessive or unvaried stress, particularly frustration, becomes distress. And this, in turn, can lead to ulcers, hypertension, and mental or physical breakdown.

In this marvelously wise and helpful book, Dr. Hans Selye, the world's leading authority on stress, gives us his prescription for minimizing the psychic insults to the nervous system, mobilizing stress for creative and idealistic purposes, and enjoying a full life in harmony with the laws of Nature.

## STRESS WITHOUT DISTRESS

### by

### HANS SELYE, M.D.

HANS SELYE, M.D., Professor and Director of the Institute of Experimental Medicine and Surgery in the University of Montreal, is best known for his work on the body's physiological response to stress, the major subject of his almost forty years of laboratory research. In addition to his doctorate in medicine, Dr. Selye holds two earned doctorates in science plus sixteen honorary degrees from universities in Europe, South America, Japan, Canada, and the United States. He has contributed over 1400 articles to technical journals and written 28 books, including *The Stress of Life*, a classic and widely acclaimed study. Dr. Selye has received numerous medals, awards, and Honorary Fellowships from scientific societies throughout the world, and has been made a Companion of the Order of Canada, his country's highest honor.

# SIGNET Books of Special Interest

*To those who try to find themselves*

# Contents

# Acknowledgments

My thanks are due first of all to Mrs. Beatrice Rosenfeld of the J. B. Lippincott Company, without whose creative editorial assistance this effort could never have bridged the gap between a typescript and a printable book. Second, to Ovid Da Silva, chief editor of the Institute of Experimental Medicine and Surgery, who, assisted by several secretaries (particularly Franca Intrevado and Danielle Charette), made a presentable manuscript out of my sloppy dictation.

Finally, I am most grateful to my colleagues and friends from all over the world—specialists in the most diverse branches of medicine, philosophy, sociology, and literature—who took the time to read and criticize the first rough draft. It would be impractical to list them all, but I have been influenced especially by: C. G. Arnold (Southington, Conn.); Z. M. Bacq (Liège); W. D. Boaz (Cleveland); G. Biörck (Stockholm); P. G. Bourne (Washington); J. Brod (Hannover-Kleefeld); M. Callaghan (Toronto); G. Carlestam (Stockholm); D. C. Clark (Hamilton); S. A. Corson (Columbus); L. Eitinger (Oslo); G. Ember (Ottawa); U. S. von Euler (Stockholm); A. C. Fonder (Rock Falls, Ill.); M. Frankenhaeuser (Stockholm); B. Gardell (Stockholm); H. Goldblatt (Cleveland); A. R. Kagan (Geneva); H. Laborit (Paris); M. H. Lader (London); E. Laszlo (Geneseo, N.Y.); R. S. Lazarus (Berkeley); L. Levi (Stockholm); H. MacLennan (Montreal); J. W. Mason (Washington); P. W. Pruyser (Topeka); L. E. Read (New York); D.

Rioch (Silver Spring, Md.); M. Tausk (Nijmegen); P. S. Timiras (Berkeley); W. H. Wehrmacher (Maywood, Ill.); H. Weiner (New York); S. Wolf (Galveston); and F. E. Yates (Los Angeles).

The medical research which provided the basis for this book was mainly subsidized by: Conseil de la recherche médicale du Québec; Medical Research Council of Canada; Ministère des affaires sociales du Québec; Fondation Canadienne des maladies du coeur; Fondation du Québec des maladies du coeur: Fondation J. A. De Sève; U.S. Army Medical Research and Development Command; Department of Health, Education and Welfare; National Library of Medicine; National Institute of Child Health and Human Development; Wyeth Laboratories; Biermans Foundation; Pfizer Foundation; Smith Kline and French Laboratories; Hoffman-La Roche Incorporated; The Population Council, New York, U.S.A.; Cancer Research, Inc.; The Canadian Tobacco Industry; The Council for Tobacco Research —U.S.A.; Colonial Research Institute; Banner Gelatin Products Corp.; John A. Hartford Foundation; and *Reader's Digest.*

*No wind favors him who has no destined port.*

—*Montaigne*

# Introduction

Almost four decades of laboratory research on the physiological mechanisms of adaptation to the stress of life have convinced me that the basic principles of defense on the cellular level are largely applicable also to people and even to entire societies of man. We shall see that the diverse biochemical adaptive reactions used by our cells and organs are surprisingly similar, irrespective of the kind of aggressor faced. This consideration led me to conceive of "physiological stress" as a response to any type of demand made on the body. Whatever the problem, it can be met only through one of two basic reaction forms: actively, through fight, or passively, by running away or putting up with it. In the case of poisons which have entered the body, flight is impossible; yet

1

our cells can still respond only in two essentially similar ways: by chemically destroying the poison, or by establishing a state of peaceful coexistence with it. Such an equilibrium can be achieved either through excretion from the body or by learning to ignore it.

Nature has foreseen innumerable reactions through which the orders to attack or to tolerate poisons can be transmitted to our cells in a chemical language. It has seemed to me that the rules which act so efficiently at the level of cells and organs could also be the source of a natural philosophy of life, leading to a code of behavior based on scientific principles, rather than on superstition, tradition, or blind subservience to the commands of any "unquestionable authority."

Throughout the centuries, all sorts of suggestions have been made about how to achieve peace and happiness through technical or political advances, higher living standards, better law enforcement, or strict adherence to the commands or teachings of a particular leader, sage, or prophet. Yet history has proven, over and over again, that none of these means is reliably efficacious.

Those who believed in the infallibility of their God or in their particular code of conduct were relatively well-balanced and happy, regardless of whether their beliefs were demonstrably correct.

At least faith gave men direction, the basis for commitment, self-discipline, and work that is indispensable to prevent abnormal chaotic behavior. Eventually, however, the convictions guiding one group of people invariably clashed with those of another, and conflicts became inevitable. The "unquestionable authority" (God, king, political leader) of one group was not only questioned but even attacked by others.

As Karl Popper says, a law of Nature is not prescriptive but descriptive. A law of society prescribes what we may or may not do. It can be broken, which is the only justification for formulating it. A law of Nature, on the other hand, merely tells us what happens under specified conditions (e.g., water boils at 100° C). At any given stage of our knowledge, it may be falsely formulated, but it cannot be broken. Scientific facts have been designated as "laws" because originally they were regarded as dictated by divine commands.

As I believe man needs more natural ideals than those which presently guide him, I have attempted to lay the foundations for a code of behavior based primarily on the laws of Nature, of which we are part and which we must all accept. This code is, at the same time, both compatible with and independent of any religion, political system, or philosophy. We are all the children of Nature

and cannot go wrong by following her general
laws in conjunction with whatever additional
personal ideals or convictions may guide us. My
creed is not concerned with the origin of life, its
creator, or the purpose of creation, but with the
ready-made human machine. It is based upon how
the body works, or how it should work—not who
created it and why, or even on the genetic code
which, in chemical language, contains the recipe
of all our traits inherited at birth. It deals only
with a strategy for optimal life after birth, irrespective of how we came into being.

My own code is based on the view that, to
achieve peace of mind and fulfillment through
self-expression, most men need a commitment to
work in the service of some cause that they can
respect. The highly motivated musician, painter,
writer, scientist, businessman, or athlete is terribly
distressed if prevented from doing his or her
work. For an active man or woman, one of the
most difficult things to bear is enforced inactivity
during prolonged hospitalization or after retirement. But let us admit that not everybody is built
this way. There are the beachcomber, the con-
stitutional loafer, the congenital pensioner, and
the person who feels happiest while passively enjoying the gifts of Nature—the sunny beaches,
the quiet forests—or the creations of others: music,
literature, or spectator sports. Such people are

satisfied to observe without actively participating. And why shouldn't they?

Of course, work and relaxation are not mutually exclusive. Most people consider their work to be their primary function in life but like to relax from time to time by a change from their occupations to hobbies or by simply enjoying what Nature or other men have to offer. The degree to which various people get satisfaction from active or passive behavior differs enormously.

I would like to dispel from the outset any thought that I consider my code to be the only way of living that can bring happiness. Far from it. People are very different, and no one formula could be equally appropriate for everybody. Let me also emphasize that I place no value judgment on particular life styles. As long as a man's pattern of behavior does not hurt others, he should live the life that is most natural to him.

However, my belief, which is based on biological laws, is that, for the great majority of people, and certainly for society as a whole, the best motive is not to "love thy neighbor as thyself" (for that is impossible), but to "*earn* thy neighbor's love." It permits you to express your talents by the most powerful means of maintaining security and peace of mind. It does so through a kind of altruistic egotism that gives expression to the inherent selfishness of living matter without causing guilt feelings; not can it be subject to attack or hostility, since it is useful to everybody.

Any code of behavior founded on biological laws must also take into account that work as such is a basic necessity of living matter, especially work whose fruits can be accumulated. The instinctive nature of this drive is shown by the very general tendency to collect (food, wealth, or even stamps, butterflies, colorful pebbles, or sea shells). He who follows our doctrine will greedily hoard wealth and strength, not in the form of money or domination of others, but by earning the goodwill, gratitude, respect, and love of those who surround him. Then, even if he has neither money nor power to command, he will still become virtually unassailable and safe, for no one would have a personal reason to attack him.

My ideas on a philosophy of gratitude were first expressed—in my book *The Stress of Life*, published in 1956 by McGraw-Hill—as afterthoughts in a much more extensive, technical discussion of stress. At that time, I did not attach much importance to such psychological considerations, since I was too preoccupied with the explication of the intricate biochemical mechanisms governing stress and the "diseases of stress" or "diseases of adaptation." Much to my surprise, these rather subjective digressions from stress as a medical problem have raised a disproportionate amount of interest among psychologists, sociologists, anthropologists, and even clergymen of different faiths. I have received at least as much mail about the philosophy of gratitude as about any of the more tangible medical subjects discussed in *The Stress of Life*. In fact, I—who had never before spoken on anything but medical subjects—have been asked to elaborate these ideas in churches and synagogues, and at conventions of such diverse groups as the Young President's Clubs, the Million Dollar Round Table, and Maharishi Mahesh Yogi's International Meditation Society.

Though my professional research and teaching commitments do not leave much time for paramedical activities, contacts with these varied groups have considerably extended and polished my own views on the philosophical implications of stress research. I came to realize that "gratitude" is only one aspect of the broader concept of love, which has been used historically to encompass all positive feelings towards others, including respect, goodwill, sympathy, and most forms of approval and admiration. Besides, since 1956, technological advances in our rapidly changing world are making more and more special demands on our abilities for readaptation. Now, through the media in our homes, we are facing daily new and often threatening events wherever they occur on earth (Vietnam, Watergate, the Middle East) or even in outer space. On the other hand, jet travel tends to make many of us feel uprooted and virtually homeless. Ever-increasing requirements for travel create the need for adaptation to different time zones, customs, languages, lodgings, and a sense of instability caused by unpredictable changes in schedules. The now almost instantaneous dissemination of disquieting news and revolutionary new ideas permeates every part of society so that a reliable code of behavior and an unchanging ideal to lean upon for support become more and more difficult to formulate.

This book will attempt to develop these thoughts, from their original expression in *The Stress of Life* to my present views, not only to update the philosophy of gratitude, but also to substantiate my creed by showing how largely it is based on general natural laws, mainly on the body's reaction to stress. This concept has helped me a great deal in keeping happily on a steady course through the many vicissitudes and uncertainties of my own long life, and I hope it can do the same for many others.

To those who are satisfied with a completely unproductive life of self-indulgence, who always drift about aimlessly, not to relax from their main pursuits but as an ultimate aim in life, I can offer no helpful advice. Mind you, I do not condemn them; it would be unbecoming for a biologist to set himself up as a judge of moral values. Yet, as far as I can see, many of these pure spectators of life are not really happy; they merely got lost, often as adolescents, because they did not give enough thought to choosing a career and setting a steady course for their lives. Still, a few of them seem to be perfectly content doing nothing constructive and living off Nature or the toil of others. They are undoubtedly vulnerable to attack, for no one has any special reason to protect them; but, in times of peace and in sheltered surroundings, they may get through life happily. In any event, for these people, the best I can do is to admit that this book is not meant for them—unless it can change their outlook on life.

The ideas to be expressed here are supported by biological research into the great laws that regulate the body's resistance to any type of injury and help to maintain life in the face of all kinds of adversity, particularly during periods of excessive stress. Hence, I must explain, at least in broad nontechnical terms, what we have learned about stress through objective laboratory experiments, in order to show how our findings might help to formulate guidelines for natural human behavior. A minimum of technical information is indispensable if this is not to be one more of those "inspirational" books relying on the writer's skill in convincing people rather than on demonstrable natural laws.

I arrived at the concepts to be outlined here by my own research on stress. Yet, in formulating my recommendations, I have also leaned heavily on previously known facts. Foremost among these are observations about the evolution of natural selfishness in living beings, their need for security and for the expression of whatever drives motivate them, the frustrating choice between seeking immediate gratification and attaining long-range goals. However, these facts are only superficially, or not at all, related to what I described as the "stress syndrome."

All these points will be touched upon throughout this book, wherever it seems most appropriate. But to start with, let us analyze the concept of biological stress, which was my main inducement for formulating the view that the best guideline to behavior is to strive for accomplishments which will *"earn* thy neighbor's love."

# 1

# The stress of life

## WHAT IS STRESS?

Everybody has it, everybody talks about it, yet few people have taken the trouble to find out what stress really is. Many words have become fashionable when scientific research revealed a new concept likely to influence our way of thinking about major issues of life or to affect our everyday conduct. Such terms as "Darwinian evolution," "allergy," and "psychoanalysis" have all had their peaks of popularity in drawing-room or cocktail-party conversations; but rarely are the opinions about them based on a study of technical works written by the scientists who established these concepts.

Nowadays, we hear a great deal at social gatherings about the stress of executive life, retirement, exercise, family problems, pollution, air traffic control, or the death of a relative. But how many of those defending their strong convictions about these matters with heated arguments have bothered to learn the scientific meaning of stress and the mechanism of its workings? Most people have never even wondered whether there is a difference between stress and distress!

The word "stress," like "success," "failure," or "happiness," means different things to different people, so that defining it is extremely difficult although it has become part of our daily vocabulary. Is stress merely a synonym for distress? It is effort, fatigue, pain, fear, the need for concentration, the humiliation of censure, the loss of blood, or even an unexpected great success which requires complete reformulation of one's entire life? The answer is yes and no. That is what makes the definition of stress so difficult. Every one of these conditions produces stress, but none of them can be singled out as being "it," since the word applies equally to all the others.

Yet, how are we to cope with the stress of life if we cannot even define it? The businessman who is under constant pressure from his clients and employees alike, the air-traffic controller who knows that a moment of distraction may mean death to hundreds of people, the athlete who desperately wants to win a race, and the husband who helplessly watches his wife slowly and painfully dying of cancer, all suffer from stress. The problems they face are totally different, but medical research has shown that in many respects the body responds in a stereotyped manner, with identical biochemical changes, essentially meant to cope with any type of increased demand upon the human machinery. The stress-producing factors—technically called *stressors*—are different, yet they all elicit essentially the same biological stress response. This distinction between stressor and stress was perhaps the first important step in the scientific analysis of that most common biological phenomenon that we all know only too well from personal experience.

But if we want to use what the laboratory has taught us about stress in formulating our own philosophy of life, if we want to avoid its bad effects and yet be able to enjoy the pleasures of accomplishment, we have to learn more about the nature and mechanism of stress. In order to succeed in this, in order to arrive at a basis for a scientific philosophy of conduct—a rational prophylactic and therapeutic science of human behavior—we must concentrate in this somewhat difficult first chapter on the fundamental technical data which the laboratory has given us.

In writing this book, it seemed logical to begin with what the physician means by the term *stress*, at the same time familiarizing the reader with the few technical expressions that are essential. (For those quite unacquainted with biology, the Glossary at the end of the book will also be of help.)

*Stress is the nonspecific response of the body to any demand made upon it.* To understand this definition we must first explain what we mean by *nonspecific*. Each demand made upon our body is in a sense unique, that is, *specific*. When exposed to cold, we shiver to produce more heat, and the blood vessels in our skin contract to diminish the loss of heat from the body surfaces. When exposed to heat, we sweat because the evaporation of perspiration from the surface of our skin has a cooling effect. When we eat too much sugar and the blood-sugar level rises above normal, we excrete some of it and burn up the rest so that the blood sugar returns to normal. A great muscular effort, such as running up many flights of stairs at full speed, makes increased demands upon our musculature and cardiovascular system. The muscles will need supplemental energy to perform this unusual work; hence, the heart will beat more rapidly and strongly, and the blood pressure will rise to dilate the vessels, thereby increasing the flow of blood to the muscles.

Each drug or hormone has such specific actions: diuretic drugs increase the production of urine; the hormone adrenalin augments the pulse rate and blood pressure, simultaneously raising blood sugar, whereas the hormone insulin decreases blood sugar. Yet, no matter what kind of derangement is produced, all these agents have one thing in common; they also increase the demand for readjustment. This demand is nonspecific; it requires adaptation to a problem, irrespective of what that problem may be.

In other words, in addition to their specific actions, all agents to which we are exposed also produce a nonspecific increase in the need to perform adaptive functions and thereby to re-establish normalcy. This is independent of the specific activity that caused the rise in requirements. The nonspecific demand for activity as such is the essence of stress.

From the point of view of its stress-producing or stressor activity, *it is immaterial whether the agent or situation we face is pleasant or unpleasant;* all that counts is the intensity of the demand for readjustment or adaptation. The mother who is suddenly told that her only son died in battle suffers a terrible mental shock; if years later it turns out that the news was false and the son unexpectedly walks into her room alive and well, she experiences extreme joy. The specific results of the two events, sorrow and joy, are completely different, in fact, opposite to each other, yet their stressor effect—the nonspecific demand to readjust herself to an entirely new situation—may be the same.

It is difficult to see how such essentially different things as cold, heat, drugs, hormones, sorrow, and joy could provoke an identical biochemical reaction in the body. Nevertheless, this is the case; it can now be demonstrated, by highly objective quantitative biochemical determinations, that certain reactions are totally nonspecific, and common to all types of exposure.

It has taken medicine a long time to accept the existence of such a stereotyped response. It did not seem logical that different tasks, in fact any task, should require the same response. Yet, if you come to think of it, there are many analogies in everyday life in which highly specific things or events share the same nonspecific feature. At first sight it is difficult to see what could be the common denominator between a man, a table, and a tree, yet they all have weight. There is no object completely devoid of weight; the pressure exerted on the scale balance does not depend upon such a specific feature as temperature, color, or shape, any more than the stressor effect of a demand upon the body depends on the kind of adaptive reaction that is required to meet it.

Or consider the appliances in a house that has heaters, refrigerators, bells, and light bulbs, which respectively produce heat, cold, sound, or light, in a most specific manner; yet to function they all depend upon one common factor—electricity. A member of a primitive tribe who never heard of electricity would find it very difficult to accept that all the manifold phenomena just mentioned depend upon the satisfaction of a common demand: the provision of electrical energy.

## WHAT STRESS IS NOT

Since the term "stress" is often used quite loosely, many confusing and contradictory definitions of it have been formulated; hence, it will be useful to add a few remarks stating clearly what it is not.

*Stress is not merely nervous tension.* This fact must be especially emphasized, since most laymen and even many scientists tend to identify biological stress with nervous exhaustion or intense emotional arousal. Indeed, quite recently, Dr. John W. Mason, a former president of the American Psychosomatic Society and one of the most distinguished investigators of the psychologic and psychiatric aspects of biological stress, devoted an excellent essay to an analysis of my stress theory. He suggested that the common denominator of stressors may simply be activation of "the physiological apparatus involved in emotional or arousal reactions to threatening or unpleasant factors in the life situation as a whole." In man, with his highly developed nervous system, emotional stimuli are in fact the most common stressors—and, of course, these would be encountered most frequently in psychiatric patients.

It must not be forgotten, however, that stress reactions do occur in lower animals that have no nervous system, and even in plants. Furthermore, the so-called stress of anesthesia is a well-recognized phenomenon in surgery, and numerous investigators have tried to eliminate this undesirable complication of the loss of consciousness.

*Stress is not always the nonspecific result of damage.* We have seen that it is immaterial whether a stressor is pleasant or unpleasant; its stressor effect depends merely on the intensity of the demand made upon the adaptive capacity of the body. Any kind of normal activity—a game of chess or even a passionate embrace—can produce considerable stress without causing harmful effects. Damaging or unpleasant stress is "distress."

The word "stress" allegedly came into common English usage, via Old French and Middle English, as "distress." The first syllable eventually was lost through slurring, as children turn "be-cause" into " 'cause." In the light of our investigations, the true meaning of the two words became totally different despite their common ancestry, just as in correct usage we distinguish between "because" (since) and "cause" (reason). Activity associated with stress may be pleasant or unpleasant; distress is always disagreeable.

*Stress is not something to be avoided.* In fact, it is evident from the definition given at the beginning of this chapter that it cannot be avoided.

In common parlance, when we say someone is "under stress," we actually mean under excessive stress or distress, just as the statement "he is running a temperature" refers to an abnormally high temperature, that is, fever. Some heat production is essential to life.

Similarly, no matter what you do or what happens to you, there arises a demand for the necessary energy required to maintain life, to resist aggression and to adapt to constantly changing external influences. Even while fully relaxed and asleep, you are under some stress. Your heart must continue to pump blood, your intestines to digest last night's dinner, and your muscles to move your chest for respiration. Even your brain is not at rest while you are dreaming.

*Complete freedom from stress is death.* That stress can be associated with pleasant or unpleasant experiences is illustrated in Figure 1. Note that the physiological stress level is lowest during indifference but never goes down to zero. (That would be death.) Pleasant as well as unpleasant emotional arousal is accompanied by an increase in physiological stress (but not necessarily in distress).

Essentially the same diagram could be used to show stress produced by different degrees of stimulation if the label "Extremely unpleasant" on the left were replaced by "Deprivation" (e.g., understimulation) and "Extremely pleasant" on the right by "Excess" (e.g., overstimulation). Ac-

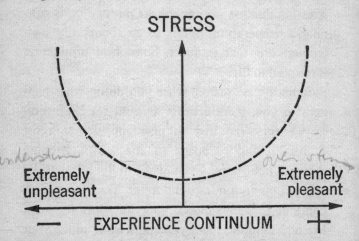

Figure 1. Theoretical model showing the relation between stress and various types of life experiences. (Courtesy L. Levi.)

cording to this hypothesis, deprivation of stimuli and excessive stimulation are both accompanied by an increase in stress, sometimes to the point of distress.

Although, contrary to public opinion, we must not—and indeed cannot—avoid stress, we can meet it efficiently and enjoy it by learning more about its mechanism and adjusting our philosophy of life accordingly. That is what this book is all about.

Perhaps the easiest way to enter into the spirit of the stress concept is to review briefly its historical development in anecdotal style.

## THE EVOLUTION OF THE STRESS CONCEPT

The concept of stress is very old. It must have occurred even to prehistoric man that the loss of vigor and the feeling of exhaustion that overcame him after hard labor, prolonged exposure to cold or heat, loss of blood, agonizing fear, or any kind of disease had something in common. He may not have been consciously aware of this similarity in his response to anything that was simply too much for him, but when the feeling came he must have realized instinctively that he had exceeded the limits of what he could reasonably handle—that, in other words, he had "had it."

Man soon must have found out also that when

he is faced with a prolonged and unaccustomed hardship—swimming in cold water, lifting rocks, or going without food—his reactions follow a pattern: at first, the experience is difficult, then one gets used to it, and finally one cannot stand it any longer. He did not think of this triphasic response as a general law regulating the behavior of living beings faced with an exacting task. The immediate necessities of finding food and shelter kept him too busy to worry about the theoretical explanations of what he was experiencing. Yet, the vague outlines of understanding were there, ready to be analyzed and translated from intuitive feelings into the precise terms of science, a language that can be appraised by intellect and tested by experiments and the critique of reason.

The greatest handicap of early students of this topic was their failure to distinguish between distress, which is always unpleasant, and the general concept of stress, which, in addition, also includes the pleasant experiences of joy, fulfillment, and self-expression.

It was the great French physiologist Claude Bernard who during the second half of the 19th century—well before anyone thought of stress—first pointed out clearly that the internal environment ( the *milieu intérieur*) of a living organism must remain fairly constant, despite changes in its external environment. He realized that "it is a fixity of the *milieu intérieur* which is the condition of free and independent life."

Some fifty years later, the distinguished American physiologist, Walter B. Cannon suggested that "the coordinated physiological processes which maintain most of the steady states in the organism" should be called "homeostasis" (from the Greek *homoios*, meaning similar, and *stasis*, meaning position), the ability to stay the same, or static. Homeostasis might roughly be translated as "staying power."

Let me explain these two related concepts a little more clearly. What is meant by the "fixity of the *milieu intérieur*"? Everything inside my skin is my *milieu intérieur*—my internal environment. In fact, the skin tissue itself is also in it. In other words, my *milieu intérieur* is me—or at least the environment in which all my cells live. In order to maintain a healthy life, nothing within me must be allowed to deviate far from the norm. If anything does, I will become sick or even die.

*The laboratory approach to the concept of nonspecificity.* Is there a nonspecific adaptive reaction to change as such? In 1926, as a second-year medical student, I first came across this problem of a stereotyped response to any exacting demand made upon the body. I began to wonder why patients suffering from the most diverse diseases that threaten homeostasis have so many signs and symptoms in common. Whether a man suffers from a severe loss of blood, an infectious disease, or advanced cancer, he loses his appetite, his muscular strength, and his ambition to accomplish anything; usually, the patient also loses weight, and even his facial expression betrays that he is ill. What is the scientific basis of what at that time I thought of as the "syndrome of just being sick"? Could the mechanism of this syndrome be analyzed by modern scientific techniques? Could it be reduced to its elements and expressed in the precise terms of biochemistry, biophysics, and morphology?

*How could different stimuli produce the same result?* In 1936, this problem presented itself again —under conditions more suited to exact laboratory analysis. It turned out in the course of my experiments in which rats were injected with various impure and toxic gland preparations that, irrespective of the tissue from which they were made or their hormone content, the injections produced a stereotyped syndrome (a set of simultaneously occurring organ changes), characterized by enlargement and hyperactivity of the adrenal cortex, shrinkage (or atrophy) of the thymus gland and lymph nodes, and the appearance of gastrointestinal ulcers.

As we have now begun to run into technical terms, let me explain a few: The adrenals are endocrine glands situated just above each kidney. They consist of two parts, the outer layer (or cortex) and the inner core (or medulla). The cortex produces hormones that I called *corticoids* (such as cortisone), whereas the medulla secretes adrenalin and related hormones, all of which play important roles in the response to stress. The thymus (a large lymphatic organ in the chest) and the lymph nodes (such as can be felt in the groins and armpits) form a single system usually referred to as the thymicolymphatic apparatus, which is mainly involved in immune defense reactions.

It soon became evident from animal experiments that the same set of organ changes caused by the glandular extracts were also produced by cold, heat, infection, trauma, hemorrhage, nervous irritation, and many other stimuli. Here was an experimental replica of the "syndrome of just being sick," a model that lent itself to quantitative appraisal; for example, now the effects of the most diverse agents could be compared in terms of the adrenal enlargement or thymus atrophy that they produced. This reaction was first described, in 1936, as a "syndrome produced by various nocuous agents" and subsequently became known as the *general adaptation syndrome (G.A.S.)*, or the *biological stress syndrome*. Its three stages—(1) the alarm reaction; (2) the stage of resistance; and (3) the stage of exhaustion—are illustrated in Figure 2.

Because of its great practical importance, it should be pointed out that the triphasic nature of the G.A.S. gave us the first indication that the body's adaptability, or *adaptation energy*, is finite. Animal experiments have shown that exposure to cold, muscular effort, hemorrhage, and other stressors can be withstood just so long. After the initial alarm reaction, the body becomes adapted and begins to resist, the length of the resistance period depending upon the body's inate adaptability and the intensity of the stressor. Yet, eventually, exhaustion ensues.

We still do not know precisely just what is lost, except that it is not merely caloric energy, since food intake is normal during the stage of resistance. Hence, one would think that once adaptation has occurred, and energy is amply available, resistance should go on indefinitely. But just as any inanimate machine gradually wears out, even if it has enough fuel, so does the human machine sooner or later become the victim of constant wear and tear. These three stages are analogous to the three stages of man's life: childhood (with its characteristic low resistance and excessive responses to any kind of stimulus), adulthood (during which adaptation to most commonly encountered agents has occurred and resistance is increased) and finally, senility (characterized by irreversible loss of adaptability and eventual exhaustion) ending with death. We shall have more to say about this later, in connection with stress and aging.

Meanwhile, although we have no precise scien-

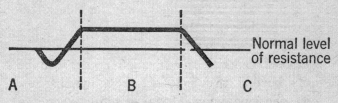

Figure 2. The three phases of the general adaptation syndrome (G.A.S.).

A. Alarm reaction. The body shows the changes characteristic of the first exposure to a stressor. At the same time, its resistance is diminished and, if the stressor is sufficiently strong (severe burns, extremes of temperature), death may result.

B. Stage of resistance. Resistance ensues if continued exposure to the stressor is compatible with adaptation. The bodily signs characteristic of the alarm reaction have virtually disappeared, and resistance rises above normal.

C. Stage of exhaustion. Following long-continued exposure to the same stressor, to which the body had become adjusted, eventually adaptation energy is exhausted. The signs of the alarm reaction reappear, but now they are irreversible, and the individual dies.

tific method for measuring adaptation energy, experiments with laboratory animals offer rather convincing evidence that the capacity for adaptation is finite. Our reserves of adaptation energy could be compared to an inherited fortune from which we can make withdrawals; but there is no proof that we can also make additional deposits. We can squander our adaptability recklessly, "burning the candle at both ends," or we can learn to make this valuable resource last long, by using it wisely and sparingly, only for things that are worthwhile and cause least distress.

As I have said, we have no objective proof that additional deposits of adaptation energy can be made beyond that inherited from our parents. Yet, everyone knows from personal experience that, after complete exhaustion by excessively stressful work during the day, a good night's sleep —and, after even more severe exhaustion, a few weeks of restful holidays—can restore our resistance and adaptability very close to what it was before. I said "very close to," because complete restoration is probably impossible, since every biologic activity leaves some irreversible "chemical scars," as we shall see later in the section "Stress and Aging." If this is the case, we must distinguish between *superficial* and *deep* adaptation energy. Superficial adaptation energy is immediately available upon demand, like money in a bank account that is readily accessible by writing out a check. On the other hand, deep adaptation energy is stored away safely as a reserve, just as part of our inherited fortune may be invested in stocks and bonds, which must first be sold to replenish our checking account, thus furnishing another supply of immediately usable cash. Still, after a lifetime of constant expenditure, even our last investments will be eventually exhausted if we only spend and never earn. I look upon the irreversible process of aging as something very similar. The stage of exhaustion, after a temporary demand upon the body, is reversible, but the complete exhaustion of all stores of deep adaptation energy is not; as these reserves are depleted, senility and, finally, death ensue.

But let us get back to the history of the stress concept and its objective analysis by laboratory experiments.

Since 1936, numerous additional biochemical and structural changes of previously unknown origin have been traced to nonspecific stress. Among these, special attention has been given by clinicians to changes in the chemical constituents of the body and to nervous reactions.

Much progress has also been made in the analysis of the hormonal mediation of stress reactions. It is now generally recognized that the emergency discharge of adrenalin represents only one aspect of the acute phase of the initial alarm reaction to stressors. At least equally important in the maintenance of homeostasis—the body's stability—is the hypothalamus-pituitary-adreno-cortical axis, which probably participates in the development of many disease phenomena as well (Figure 3). This "axis" is a coordinated system consisting of the hypothalamus (a brain region at the base of the skull) that is connected with the pituitary gland (hypophysis), which regulates adrenocortical activity. The stressor excites the hypothalamus (through pathways not yet fully identified) to produce a substance that stimulates the pituitary to discharge the hormone ACTH (for *a*dreno-*c*ortico*t*rophic *h*ormone) into the blood. ACTH in turn induces the external, cortical portion of the adrenal to secrete corticoids. These elicit thymus shrinkage, simultaneously with many other changes, such as atrophy of the lymph nodes, inhibition of inflammatory reactions, and production of sugar (a readily available source of energy). Another typical feature of the stress reaction is the development of peptic ulcers in the stomach and intestine. Their production is facilitated through an increased level of corticoids in the blood, but the autonomic nervous system also plays a role in eliciting ulcers.

The history of the G.A.S. suggests that the key to real progress was the discovery of objective

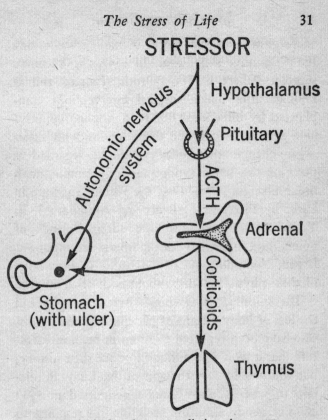

Figure 3. Principal pathways mediating the response to a stressor

indices of stress, such as adrenal enlargement, thymus atrophy, and gastrointestinal ulcers. But even these signs were known to some physicians long before anyone realized that there is such a thing as a nonspecific stress syndrome. As early as 1842, the British physician Thomas B. Curling described acute gastrointestinal ulcers in patients who suffered extensive skin burns. In 1867, the Viennese surgeon Albert C. T. Billroth reported similar findings after major surgical interventions complicated by infections. But there was no conceivable reason to connect these lesions with other organ changes that today would be regarded as parts of the stress syndrome, for example, with organ changes observed at the Pasteur Institute in Paris, by Pierre P. E. Roux and Alexandre J. E. Yersin, who noted that the adrenal glands of guinea pigs infected with diphtheria are often enlarged, bloodshot, and hemorrhagic. In fact, none of these physicians knew about each other's work.

The so-called "accidental" thymus atrophy and the loss of body weight of patients affected by disease have been reported so often in medical literature that it would be difficult to trace their history; but who would have thought of them, say, in relation to what Walter Cannon designated in 1932 as "emergency adrenalin secretion" in response to fear or rage?

Yet, Cannon went even further. In his classic book, *The Wisdom of the Body*, he summarized his lifework on the distinct mechanisms which maintain the normalcy of sugar, protein, fat, calcium, oxygen, and temperature of the blood, as well as many other individual specific adaptive mechanisms. Thus, he laid the basis for a systematic analysis of the separate adaptive phenomena indispensable for the maintenance of life under special conditions. However, he never touched upon the role of the pituitary or the adrenal cortex; hence, it would have been difficult for him to explore the possible existence of nonspecific adaptive reactions that could play a part in coping with virtually any kind of demand.

Thus, one important link was still missing: the link connecting all these scattered observations on different agents and different results as merely individual manifestations of a single coordinated syndrome.

*How could the same reaction produce different lesions?* There remained two apparently insurmountable obstacles in the way of formulating the concept of a single stereotyped response to stress:

1. Qualitatively different stimuli of equal toxicity (or stressor potency) do not necessarily elicit exactly the same syndrome in different people.
2. Even the same degree of stress, induced by the same stimulus, may produce different lesions in different individuals.

It took many years to show that qualitatively distinct stimuli differ only in their specific actions.

Their nonspecific stressor effects are essentially the same, unless these happen to be modified by the superimposed specific effects of a particular evocative stimulus.

On the other hand, the fact that even the same stressor can cause different lesions in different individuals has been traced to "conditioning factors" that can selectively enhance or inhibit one or the other stress effect. Thus conditioning may be internal (for example, genetic predisposition, age, or sex) or external (treatment with certain hormones, drugs, or dietary factors). Under the influence of such conditioning factors (which determine sensitivity), a normally well-tolerated degree of stress can become pathogenic and cause "diseases of adaptation," selectively affecting the predisposed body area.

As illustrated by Figure 4, every agent possesses both stressor and specific effects. The former are nonspecific by definition, being common to diverse stimuli, whereas the latter are variable and characteristic of each individual agent. However, the response does not depend exclusively upon these two actions of the stimulus; the reactivity of the target also plays a role and this can be modified by numerous internal or external conditioning factors. Thus, it is clear that, since all stressors have some specific effects, they cannot always elicit exactly the same response, and even the same stimulus will act differently in different individuals, depending upon the internal and external conditioning factors which determine how each will react.

The concept of conditioning, in the sense just outlined, and the hypothesis that certain diseases are caused by derailments of the G.A.S. mechanism, have clarified the relations between the physiology and pathology of stress in many fields.

As we have seen, any kind of activity sets our stress mechanism in motion, though it will largely depend upon the accidental conditioning factors whether the heart, kidney, gastrointestinal tract, or brain will suffer most. In the body, as in a chain, the weakest link breaks down under stress although all parts are equally exposed to it.

Of course, every disease causes a certain amount of stress, since it imposes demands for adaptation upon the organism. In turn, stress plays some role in the development of every disease; its effects—for better or worse—are added to the specific changes characteristic of the disease in question. That is why the effect of stress may be curative (as in the case of various forms of shock therapy, physical therapy, occupational therapy) or damaging, depending on whether the biochemical reactions characteristic of stress (for example, stress hormones or nervous reactions to stress) combat or accentuate the trouble. All these problems have

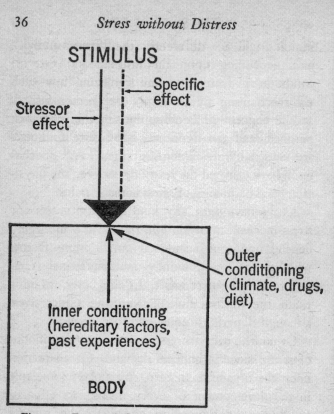

Figure 4. Factors influencing the response to stressors

been discussed at length elsewhere, both in technical and non-technical terms. (In case you wish to explore these aspects of stress, the bibliography at the end of this book lists many key references.) Suffice it to mention here that some diseases in which stress usually plays a particularly important role are high blood pressure, cardiac accidents, gastric or duodenal ulcers (the "stress ulcers"), and various types of mental disturbances.

There are many complex stabilizing biochemical mechanisms which ensure our homeostasis. It would lead us too far from the scope of this book to discuss all these in detail. But before commenting on some practical lessons taught us by research on these equilibrating responses of the body, it is necessary to mention a few additional basic facts.

*Syntoxic and catatoxic responses.* The biochemical analysis of the stress syndrome showed that homeostasis depends mainly upon two types of reactions: syntoxic (from the Greek *syn*, meaning together) and catatoxic (from the Greek *cata*, meaning against). Apparently, in order to resist different toxic stressors, the body can regulate its reactions through chemical messengers and nervous stimuli which either pacify or incite to fight. The syntoxic stimuli act as tissue tranquilizers, creating a state of passive tolerance which permits a kind of symbiosis, or peaceful coexistence with aggressors. The catatoxic agents cause chemical changes mainly through the production of destructive enzymes, which actively attack the disease producer (pathogen), usually by accelerating its degradation in the body.

Presumably, in the course of evolution, living beings have learned to defend themselves against all kinds of assaults (whether arising in the body or coming from its environment) through two basic mechanisms which help us put up with aggressors (syntoxic) or destroy them (catatoxic). Among the most effective syntoxic hormones are the corticoids. The best known members of this group are the anti-inflammatory corticoids, such as cortisone and its artificial synthetic derivatives, which inhibit inflammation and many essentially defensive immune reactions. These are being effectively used in the treatment of diseases in which inflammation itself is the major cause of trouble (e.g., certain types of inflammation of the joints, eyes, or respiratory passages). Likewise, they have a marked inhibitory effect on the immunologic rejection of grafted foreign tissues (e.g., a heart or kidney transplant).

Now it may not be immediately evident why it should be advantageous to inhibit inflammation or the rejection of foreign grafts, since both phenomena are essentially useful defense reactions. The main purpose of inflammation is to localize irritants (for example, microbes) by putting a barricade of inflammatory tissue around them. This prevents their spread into the blood, which could lead to blood poisoning and death. However, the suppression of this basic defense reaction is an advantage when a foreign agent is in itself innocuous but acts as an *agent provocateur*, causing trouble only by inciting inflammation. Here, inflammation itself is what we experience as a disease. Thus, in many patients who suffer from hay fever or extreme inflammatory swelling after an insect sting, suppression of defensive inflammation is essentially a cure. This is because the invading stressor agent is not in itself dangerous or likely to spread and kill. In the case of grafts, it may even be lifesaving.

At this point, it is useful to distinguish between direct and indirect pathogens. The former cause disease irrespective of our body's reaction, whereas the latter produce damage only through the exaggerated and purposeless defensive responses they provoke. If a patient accidentally exposes his hand to a strong acid, alkali, or boiling water, damage will occur irrespective of his reactions, because all these are direct pathogens; they would cause damage even to the body of a dead man who obviously could not put up any vital defense reactions. On the other hand, most common inflammatory irritants, including allergens, are essentially indirect pathogens, which do not themselves cause disease, but are damaging only by stimulating an inopportune and harmful fight against what is innocuous.

During evolution, immunologic reactions, which led to destruction of microbes, grafts, and other foreign tissues, developed undoubtedly as useful protective mechanisms against potentially dangerous foreign materials. However, when—as in the case of many allergens, heart transplants, etc.—the attack against the "foreign agent" is unnecessary or harmful, man can do better than Nature by suppressing this hostility.

On the other hand, when the aggressor is dangerous, the defensive reaction should not be suppressed; on the contrary, we must try to increase it above the normal level. This can be done, for example, by catatoxic substances, which carry the chemical order for our tissues to attack the invaders even more actively than would normally be the case.

We shall deal with interpersonal relations later, but here, an example from daily life will illustrate in principle how diseases can be produced indirectly by our own inappropriate or excessive adaptive reactions. If you meet a helpless drunk who showers you with insults but is obviously quite unable to do you harm, nothing will happen if you take a "syntoxic" attitude—go past and ignore him. However, if you respond catatoxically and fight, or even only prepare to fight, the result may be tragic. You will discharge adrenalin-type hormones, which increase blood pressure and pulse rate, while your whole nervous system will become alarmed and tense in preparation for combat.

If you happen to be a coronary candidate (because of age, arteriosclerosis, obesity, a high blood-cholesterol level), the result may be a fatal brain hemorrhage or heart attack. In this case, who was the murderer? The drunk didn't even touch you. This is biological suicide! Death is caused by choosing the wrong reaction.

If, on the other hand, the man who showers you with insults is a homicidal maniac with a dagger in his hand, evidently determined to kill you, it is essential to take an aggressive catatoxic attitude. You must try to disarm him even at the risk of injury to yourself by the physical accompaniments of the alarm reaction in preparation for combat. It is clear, then, that Nature, contrary to general opinion, does not always know best. Both on the cellular and interpersonal level, we do not always recognize what is and what is not worth fighting.

*Can we improve on Nature's own defenses?* The "Nature knows best" theory seems to be particularly obvious in the case of adaptive reactions. It is assumed that, in the millions of years of adaptation since life first appeared on this globe, gradually the laws of natural selection by "survival of the fittest" have worked out the best possible defense reactions. This is far from true. We can often improve upon Nature by suppressing responses which were apparently developed for defense, but which are not necessarily useful under all circumstances.

For that matter, the concept of the survival of the fittest has been abused to justify the principle of "Might is right." We must be careful to understand that "fittest" does not mean "strongest." Darwin himself was bitter about his theory being misused to justify every kind of fraudulent business, inhuman cruelty, or warfare against the weak to accelerate evolution.

While we know a great deal about the body's capacity to produce syntoxic hormones, such as corticoids, which induce a desired state of peaceful coexistence with various pathogens, we know substantially less about the ability of our organism to produce catatoxic substances. Some natural hormones do possess such activities, but they are weak. The most active catatoxic compounds are synthetics. The most powerful among these is a hormone derivative designated by the chemical name "pregnenolone-16α-carbonitrile" (PCN). Among those so far examined, it is most potent, and most nonspecific in that it exhibits the greatest destructive ability against the largest number of poisons.

These compounds provide defense against aggressors within the organism, such as toxic chemicals produced by the body or introduced into it. But what about defense against assaults by other people? Here, the syntoxic mechanism is still applicable because many a troublesome situation can be avoided if you merely learn consciously to ignore it, as in the previously mentioned example of dealing with a helpless drunk. On the other hand, classic catatoxic mechanisms (as described above) are obviously not suitable since you cannot chemically disintegrate your enemies by destructive enzymes made in your body. Yet, in essence, here also, catatoxic reactions are usable if we interpret the word in its original meaning of attacking the foe without specifying by what means. We can attempt to assault and disarm him. Finally, we can run away. So, when it comes to interpersonal defense reactions, three possibilities exist: (1) the syntoxic, which ignores the enemy and puts up with him without trying to attack him; (2) the catatoxic, which results in a fight; and (3) flight, an attempt to escape from the enemy without either putting up with him or trying to destroy him. This last possibility obviously does not apply in the fight against poisons inside the body.

These remarks on interpersonal relations give us the first inkling of the close connection that exists between adaptive and defensive reactions on a cellular level within the organism, and between different people or even groups of people.

At first sight, it is odd that the laws governing life's responses at such different levels as a cell, a whole person, or even a nation should be so essentially similar. Yet this type of simplicity and uniformity characterizes all great laws of Nature. For example, in the inanimate world, arrangement of matter and energy in orbits circulating around a center is typical of the largest celestial bodies as well as of individual atoms. Why is it that, on these opposite levels, the large satellites circling a planet and the minute electrons around an atomic nucleus should both travel in orbits? Why is it that every object in this world consists of different combinations of the same small number of only about one hundred natural atoms?

We find comparable similarities in the great laws governing living matter. Actually, the two main problems of life are maintenance of the species and maintenance of the individual. The former is assured through the genetic code (arrived at by evolution) which—using only a few "chemical letters" (molecules)—can write out the entire recipe for the subsequent development of a living being. The same chemical alphabet is used to make a microbe, a mouse, or a man. The difference is only in the arrangement of the letters. Astonishing as this may seem, it is not so different from the structure of a language: every English word can be written by putting together, in proper order, some of the twenty-six letters of the alphabet. Everything I have written in this book—and even words not yet in use—can be unambiguously expressed in this code and placed, each in its unquestionably correct position, within a dictionary.

After a new living being has arrived in this world, there is not much you can do about his inherited characteristics, but he is immediately exposed to a hostile environment to which you can help him adjust. In his mother's womb, he was largely protected against most things, but after the umbilical cord is cut, he is on his own—exposed to cold, heat, potentially dangerous food, microbes, and physical injury. From then on, and throughout life, his major problem will be adaptation, that is, the maintenance of homeostasis. It is this, the second of the two main problems of life, that has occupied our research group ever since the discovery of the stress syndrome.

*Raising the body's thermostat of defense.* As we have seen, homeostasis largely depends upon the appropriate production of syntoxic and catatoxic agents by the body, in response to potential pathogens which threaten the fixity of the *milieu intérieur* and, hence, of survival. We can improve upon these remedies of Nature by synthesizing them (or substances like them that are even more effective) and adjusting their balance in the body to meet its requirements. In other words, in all such instances, benefit depends either upon the appropriate spontaneous production of these substances by the body or (when this is faulty) upon the corrective administration of similar defensive compounds by the physician.

A natural mechanism is usually adequate to maintain a normal state of resistance; however, when faced with unusually heavy demands, ordinary homeostasis is not enough. The "thermostat of defense" must be raised to a heightened level. For this process, I proposed the term "heterostasis" (heteros, meaning other; *stasis*, meaning position) as the establishment of a new steady state by treatment with agents which stimulate the physiological adaptive mechanisms through the development of normally dormant defensive tissue reactions. Both in homeostasis and in heterostasis, the *milieu intérieur* participates actively.

We can stimulate the production of natural protective agents, for example, by treatment with chemicals that augment the induction of catatoxic or syntoxic enzymes, or by immunization with bacterial products which increase the manufacture by the body of serological antibodies against infections (e.g., by vaccination).

In homeostatic defense, the potential pathogen (which threatens the fixity of the *milieu intérieur*) automatically sets into motion usually adequate catatoxic or syntoxic mechanisms; when these do not suffice, such natural catatoxic or syntoxic agents can also be administered ready-made by the physician. Heterostasis depends upon treatment with artificial remedies which have no direct curative action, but which can teach the body to produce unusually high amounts of its own natural catatoxic or syntoxic agents so as to achieve fixity of the *milieu intérieur*, despite abnormally high demands that could not be met without outside help.

The most salient difference between homeostasis and heterostasis is that the former maintains a normal steady state by physiological means, whereas the latter "resets the thermostat" of resis-

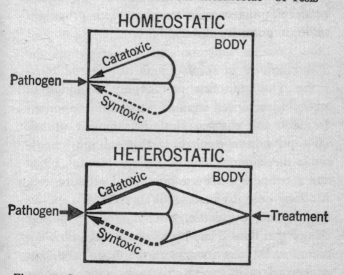

Figure 5. Comparison of homeostatic and heterostatic defense mechanisms.

tance of a heightened capacity for defense by artificial intervention from the outside (Figure 5).

All this comes down to teaching the body by
chemical treatment how to raise the production of
its own natural nonspecific (multipurpose) remedies. However, each type of intellectual teaching,
or planned and enforced physical training, also
raises resistance from the homeostatic to the heterostatic level, through outside interventions.

Heterostasis differs essentially from treatment
with drugs (e.g., antibiotics, antacids, antidotes,
pain killers) which act directly and specifically,
rather than by strengthening the body's natural
nonspecific defenses; in treatment with drugs, the
*milieu intérieur* is passive.

*The relativity of specificity in disease and treat-
ment.* The very first part of my definition of
stress characterized it as a "nonspecific response."
In discussing the historical development of this
concept, I have emphasized that specific homeostatic mechanisms for the maintenance of blood
sugar, temperature, pulse rate, blood pressure, etc.,
had long been explored by Walter Cannon and his
school; and, of course, specific remedies against
this or that disease had been known since time im-
memorial. My own work, on the other hand, was
concerned mainly with the nonspecific response
of the body to *any* demand made upon it—the

stereotyped reaction to whatever type of adaptive process is required.

Analysis of the biochemical mechanism of nonspecific homeostasis showed that these nonspecific homeostatic responses depended primarily on the automatic adjustment of the manufacture by the body of "stress hormones," through feedback mechanisms which adjust supply to demand. As we have seen, heterostasis merely helps the body to reset these feedback mechanisms to a higher level through interventions from the outside. Thereby, the body's own normally dormant capacities for producing defensive compounds are raised to levels far above those required for resistance to commonly encountered demands.

The defensive hormones (particularly the syntoxic corticoids and the chemically related catatoxic hormone derivatives, such as PCN) share the property of increasing resistance to a great many potentially pathogenic agents. They are nonspecific, multipurpose remedies, but only for the particular variety of agents against which they can protect. However, nothing is completely nonspecific; there is no such thing as a cure-all. It must be clearly understood, therefore, that specificity and nonspecificity, both in disease and in treatment, are relative concepts.

In speaking about stress in relation to homeostasis, heterostasis, and the diseases of adaptation,

I have always emphasized the nonspecific element because of its broad implications. Yet, in the preceding section, I mentioned as an example of heterostasis the awakening of the body's ability to produce immunologic antibodies. Most of these antibodies are highly specific, but some are more or less nonspecific in offering protection against various diseases. However, the production of all of them depends on homeostatic feedback mechanisms, since the demand itself triggers the manufacture of the particular curative compound that is required. Of course, through heterostasis we can also induce the production of protective antibodies in animals, but if the resulting products are then injected into patients who need them, this is no longer heterostasis but ordinary drug therapy, as is treatment with antibiotics, antidotes, cardiac stimulants, and other remedies of varying degrees of specificity.

We have also seen how the same hormone or reaction can produce different lesions through concurrent treatment with "conditioning agents," which direct the stimulus to act in qualitatively different ways and on different organs. It is this close intertwining of the specific and nonspecific that has always represented—and I am afraid in many quarters still represents—the greatest conceptual hurdle to the full understanding of modern concepts about stress and distress. The main point to understand is that heterostasis, in the sense just outlined, represents an excellent example of how to teach the body to raise its resistance and to adapt, using clearly identifiable chemical instructors. This furnishes a very tangible objective basis for discussions to come, which try to show that the roots of our recommendations for human behavior can be traced back to the molecular and cellular level. In other words, the laws of self-preservation, as exemplified by the chemical feedback mechanisms regulating resistance to nonspecific stress (and even to some specific agent), are inherent in the subcellular structure of all living organisms and, hence, furnish natural guidelines for behavior in daily life.

First of all, if you are to attempt an outline for a natural philosophy of behavior, you must ask yourself, "What does, or should, motivate my conduct?" and "What is the aim of life?" In fact, has life any "aim" other than to continue its existence, and what is the meaning of "aim" in this context?

# 2

# Motivation

A MOTIVE is "something within a person (as need, idea, organic state or emotion) that incites him to action." Synonyms: "impulse, incentive, inducement, spur. . . ."

—*Webster's Third New International Dictionary*

Living beings are motivated by a variety of impulses, among which the selfish desire to maintain oneself, to stay alive and happy, is one of the most important. The satisfaction of our instinctive drives, the need for self-expression, the impulse to collect wealth and acquire power, or to do some constructive work, to fulfill whatever *we* consider our purpose, and many other motives are conjointly responsible for our actions. It is therefore healthy to take stock of these desires and to analyze their justification and biological value in maintaining our homeostasis, our equilibrium, within ourselves and within society.

## REFLECTIONS ON EGOTISM

Egotism or selfishness is the most ancient characteristic feature of life. From the simplest microorganism to man, all living beings must protect their own interests first of all. We can hardly expect someone else to look after us more conscientiously than after himself. Selfishness is natural but, since it is considered to be ugly, we try to deny its existence in ourselves. It is also dangerous to society. We are afraid of it because it harbors the seeds of fight and revenge. Furthermore, curiously, despite our inborn egotism, many of us are strongly motivated by altruistic feelings. Yet, these two apparently contradictory impulses are not incompatible; the instinct for self-preservation need not conflict with the wish to help others. Altruism can be regarded as a modified form of egotism, a kind of collective selfishness that helps the community in that it engenders gratitude. By making another person wish that we should prosper because of what we have done—and, hence, are likely to do for him again—we elicit goodwill. This is perhaps the most humane way of assuring our security (homeostasis) in society. It abolishes the clash between our selfish and selfless tendencies. By creating gratitude and trust we induce others to share our natural wish for our own well-being. The less a person knows about the ecology of living beings, the more is he repulsed by this philosophy. I do not feel competent to question the wisdom of Nature; I merely want to analyze and understand her mechanisms.

Most people sincerely wish to be useful to society. That is why, even among those who do "pure basic research," few of us are completely indifferent to the possibility that our discoveries may help to relieve suffering and improve the quality of life.

Now let us see how egotism has been gradually transformed into a kind of altruism designed for survival.

*The evolution of altruistic egotism.* To explain the biological roots of altruistic egotism is actually the main purpose of this book. It is the basis of my creed that to earn goodwill and appreciation of our actions is the only scientific foundation for a natural code that gives us guidelines of conduct, satisfactory both to ourselves and to society, whatever lucky chances or adversities fate may have in store for us. It supplies a purpose of unquestionable value, and I would consider it the major accomplishment of my life if I could present the case for altruistic egotism so clearly and convincingly as to make it the motto for human ethics in general.

I believe that the potentially explosive and dangerous, but inevitable, drive of egotism has been gradually defused by a marriage with altruism and that the resulting altruistic egotism can lead to mutually satisfactory peaceful cooperation between competitive cells, organs, people, and even entire societies.

*Collaboration among cells.* Much of what we find in textbooks about the evolution of life on this planet is still debatable. It is safe to assume, however, that at first there was only inanimate matter, consisting of more or less disorderly arrangements of atoms and molecules. These often collided and interfered with each other, but they could hardly have had any personal interest in getting the better of their competitors. They did not "mind" being exploited; they did not feel either pride in victories due to their strength to push or shame for being pushed about. They had no "wish" to maintain their individual integrity. Despite all the turbulence associated with the birth of this planet, its constituent particles faced none of the problems that we now encounter in connection with peace and war, victory and defeat, survival and extinction.

However, as the first living unit emerged, it was confronted with such problems. Obviously, it would have disappeared had it not been able to maintain itself and perpetuate its species within a potentially competitive and even hostile environment. Eventually, it had to come to grips not only with the dangerous elements of its inanimate environment but also with other living beings, with which it was forced to compete for space, nourishment, and everything else necessary for life, at least everything of which there was an increasingly limited supply.

The great capacity for adaptation is what makes life possible on all levels of complexity. It is the basis of homeostasis and of resistance to stress. In the Foreword to my first encyclopedic treatise, *Stress,* I have tried to express this thought by saying:

> *Adaptability is probably the most distinctive characteristic of life.*
> In maintaining the independence and individuality of natural units, none of the great forces of inanimate matter are as successful as that alertness and adaptability to change which we designate as life—and the loss of which is death. Indeed there is perhaps even a certain parallelism between the

degree of aliveness and the extent of adaptability in every animal—in every man.

There are two roads to survival: fight and adaptation. And most often adaptation is the more successful.

Even adaptation can reach various degrees of perfection. The crudest form is mutual indifference, in which cells simply get out of one another's way. Up to a point, this is enough. Mutual indifference permits coexistence but not cooperation. It prevents war but provides no positive gain for any one individual, such as acquiring neighbors who might actually help; also, it offers no protection against overcrowding, with the consequent exhaustion of available living space and vital supplies.

This is probably why, in the course of evolution, colonies of individual cells got together to form a single cooperative community in which competition was amply overcompensated by mutual assistance because each member of the group could depend upon the others for help. Different cells specialized, each to undertake different functions, some to look after food intake and digestion, others to provide the means for respiration, locomotion and defense, still others to coordinate the activities of the entire colony. Among the individual cells of such closely knit complex bodies, egotism and altruism became virtually synonymous; there can be no motive for competitive struggles among cells which depend upon one another and share everything, even a single life. In fact, the evolution of diverse species was largely dependent upon the development of processes that permitted many cells to live in harmony, with a minimum of stress between them, serving their own best interests by ensuring the survival of the entire complex structure.

The development of such a sophisticated system of mutual aid between the parts of a single organism minimizes internal stress; that is, it minimizes the demands made on the organism for the avoidance of internal frictions so as to permit a harmonious coexistence of all parts of the unit.

The indispensability of this disciplined, orderly mutual cooperation is best illustrated by its opposite—the development of a cancer, whose most characteristic feature is that it cares only for itself. Hence, it feeds on the other parts of its own host until it kills the host—and thus commits biological suicide, since a cancer cell cannot live except within the body in which it started its reckless, egocentric development.

*Collaboration among separate living beings.* Still later, there also developed an interdependence (symbiosis, mutualism) between two or more individuals of completely different species. This form of mutually useful altruistic egotism is extremely widespread in Nature; one could enumerate countless examples of it, but a few will suffice.

There are instances of symbiosis between various microorganisms as well as between bacteria and higher animals. The normal bacteria that live in the intestines of a mammal not only reduce the dead bodies of ingested plants and animals to a form usable by the host, but also provide their host with an immunity to disease-producing bacteria that is lacking in animals artificially kept in a germ-free atmosphere.

Lichens, which thrive in extremely stressful environments where no other plants can survive, are unique in that they actually represent the combination of two entirely different but interdependent individuals: an alga and a fungus. They look like one single plant and always grow in association. It was only after the discovery of the microscope that the two individual members could be identified as separate beings. Their extraordinary resistance to stress is due to the fact that the metabolic processes of the alga and the fungus complement each other. The fungus provides support and water for the alga, which in turn furnishes food to the fungus.

The roots of peas, beans, and other leguminous plants, especially in arid regions, penetrate very deeply into the soil, where small swellings develop on them. These nodules house nitrogen-fixing bacteria. The excess nitrogenous compounds made by the bacteria are used by the green plant for growth; thus, landlord and tenant are interdependent.

Coral polyps contain myriads of microscopic algae upon which they rely for absorbing their own waste products. Without this self-contained sewage disposal system, the number of polyps that could live on a reef tract would be very limited.

Perhaps one of the most charming collaborative schemes of this kind is that developed by some hermit crabs. Since this type of crab has a soft, very vulnerable abdomen, it seeks protection by thrusting its body into an empty snail shell. Then it decorates its "house" with hydroids or sea anemones, sessile (attached) animals that resemble plants. The advantage to the guests is that the crab supplies them with locomotion and hence with access to a greater variety of food than would be otherwise within their reach. The advantage to the crab lies in the protective camouflage offered by its guests. The original inhabitant of the snail shell, being dead, loses nothing by this complex system of coexistence.

One could mention many similar associations among all sorts of species along the evolutionary scale. As for the individuals within a single species, the life of bees, ants, termites, and other social animals could never have reached its present stage of sophisticated development without division of labor and collaboration.

But, of course, from our point of view, the most interesting interdependence that has developed in the course of evolution is that among human beings; each of us has his own ambitions and requirements, which often clash and become the major source of interpersonal stress. Naturally, the best solution to this problem would be perfect teamwork and mutual understanding, but, despite all the codes of conduct offered by various religions, philosophies, and political systems, interpersonal relations remain very unsatisfactory. The stress of living with one another still represents one of the greatest causes of distress.

Man's central nervous system, especially his brain, is better developed than that of any other living being; this has helped considerably in solving many problems of survival through the logic of intellect. However, in interpersonal relations, we tend to be much less readily guided by logic than by emotions. Though decisions based on logic are safer, it is emotion that induces a man to sacrifice his life for his country, to marry for love, to commit sadistic crimes, or to join a religious order; he uses logic—if at all—only afterward, to rationalize the emotional act and to pursue his course more efficiently.

*Collaboration among societies.* I have already given several examples of collaboration among animals of different species and the formation of societies which assume a corporate individuality that defends its own interests against other cooperative groups. The same type of association is true, of course, in the case of human beings who collaborate on the level of the family, the clan, the tribe, the nation, or even the federation of nations whose efficiency, through the increasing strength of collaborative teamwork, is becoming more and more obvious. The many federations of geographic or ethnic groups in the U.S.A., U.S.S.R., India, China, Canada, Czechoslovakia, Yugoslavia, Switzerland, and several other countries—as long as the subunits accept living by altruistic egotism—are certainly stronger and more capable of maintaining harmonious atmospheres than each of the separate constituent parts, among which competition and struggle could break out at any time.

It is interesting that a century ago, Claude Bernard—who first called attention to the vital necessity of maintaining the stability of the body's *milieu intérieur*—devoted the last section of his famous book, *Introduction to the Study of Experi-*

*mental Medicine,* to the philosophical and social aspects of this subject.

Walter Cannon, who coined the term homeostasis, recognized the adaptive functions of adrenalin and of the sympathetic nervous system, thereby furnishing one of the most important precursors of the stress concept. It is probably no coincidence that the epilogue to his *Wisdom of the Body* is entitled "Relations of Biological and Social Homeostasis." Here, he expressed his conviction that the behavior and philosophy of man should and could be guided, to a large extent, by biological research. "Might it not be useful," he asked, "to examine other forms of organization—industrial, domestic or social—in the light of the organization of the body?" After reviewing various philosophical and political systems designed to maintain the homeostasis necessary for the happiness of mankind, he concluded that "the multiplicity of these schemes is itself proof that no satisfactory single scheme has been suggested by anybody."

I fully agree with Cannon when he says that the greatest advantage of developing specialized organs in complex living beings, including man, is that each part can better concentrate on its own special activity (locomotion, digestion, excretion of waste products) if it is supplied, through the blood stream, with the general necessities for life (oxygen, energy-yielding nutrients). However, this advantage becomes possible only if other systems coordinate all specialized activities through chemical messengers (particularly hormones) carried in the blood, and through nervous impulses harmonized by the feedback mechanisms of the central nervous system that show where there is an excess or an unsatisfied demand.

The same principles must govern cooperation between entire nations: just as a person's health depends on the harmonious conduct of the organs within his body, so must the relations between individual people, and by extension between the members of families, tribes, and nations, be harmonized by the emotions and impulses of altruistic egotism that automatically ensure peaceful cooperation and remove all motives for revolutions and wars.

In more precise and scientific terms, all this comes down to the application of what Ervin Laszlo called "systems philosophy," based on cybernetics (the science of communication and control systems in living organisms and machines) by feedback mechanisms, that is, to adaptive self-organization and homeostasis on all levels of individual and social life.

## THE OPTIMAL STRESS LEVEL

Among all the emotions, those that—more than any others—account for the absence or presence of harmful stress (distress) in human relations are the feelings of gratitude and goodwill and their negative counterparts, hatred with the urge for revenge.

Actually, such strong positive or negative feelings toward others are associated with *conditioned reflexes*, which were explored initially by the Russian physiologist Ivan Petrovich Pavlov. Unlike innate natural reactions, conditioned reflexes are acquired as a result of repeated association and training. We learn from experience to avoid whatever stimulates negative emotions or leads to punishment and to adopt a pattern of behavior that creates positive emotions and encourages reward.

On the cellular level, learning by experience depends mainly upon *chemical conditioning*, by the production of defensive substances (e.g., hormones, antibodies) and the modification of their action by other chemicals (e.g., nutrients).

Furthermore, in our experiments, we have seen many examples showing that *a brief period of exposure to stress may result in a gain or a loss*. This is amenable to scientific study because it can be assessed objectively by measurable evidence of physiological resistance. When the whole body is exposed briefly to intense stress, the result may be either beneficial (as in shock therapy) or damaging (as in a state of shock). When only part of the body is thus exposed, the result can be increased local resistance (adaptation, inflammation), or tissue breakdown, depending largely upon circumstances. We have found that the response to the stressor is directed in the body by a system of opposing forces, such as corticoids that combat or promote inflammation, and nerve impulses producing adrenalin or acetylcholine. As previously mentioned, we have also learned to distinguish between syntoxic and catatoxic compounds which respectively represent orders to tolerate or to attack.

We have learned that there is a stereotyped physical pattern of the body's response to stress of any cause. The outcome of our interactions with the environment depends just as much upon our reactions to the stressor as upon the nature of the stressor itself. We must choose carefully between efforts to resist the challenge or to disregard it by merely submitting to it.

We have discussed at some length the medical aspects of these complex interrelations between the chemical challenges to which we are exposed and the responses of our body to them. Mental stress due to interrelations between men and to their balanced satisfactory position within society is regulated by a surprisingly similar mechanism. At some point, there invariably develops a clash of interests which acts as a stressor, and there are balancing impulses for resistance or tolerance. The laws which regulate the involuntary biochemical responses within our body during stress are virtually identical with those governing voluntary interpersonal behavior.

We have seen that, depending upon our reactions, meeting a challenge may result in a gain or loss, and it is largely within our power to respond constructively once we know the rules of the game. On the automatic, involuntary level, the gain is accomplished through chemical responses (immunity, destruction of poisons, healing of wounds, etc.) which ensure survival and minimal tissue damage under a given set of circumstances. These reactions are either spontaneous or they must be guided by an experienced physician. In interpersonal stress, anybody can be (and usually has to be) his own doctor, with the help of a sound natural philosophy of conduct.

There are great individual differences in the amount of stress a person needs for happiness. But those who are content to live a purely passive vegetable life are quite exceptional. Even the least ambitious are rarely satisfied with a minimum living standard, providing only such essentials as food, shelter, and clothing.

The vast majority of mankind needs much more than that. However, those who are totally committed to some ideal and are willing to sacrifice their whole lives to achieve excellence through unique accomplishments in fields which require extraordinary mental capacities and persistence (science, art, philosophy) are perhaps just as rare as the vegetable type. Most of mankind falls between these two extremes.

The average citizen would suffer just as much from the boredom of purposeless subsistence as from the inevitable fatigue created by the constant compulsive pursuit of perfection; in other words, the majority equally dislike a lack of stress and an excess of it. Hence each of us must carefully analyze himself and try to find the particular stress level at which he feels most comfortable, whatever occupation he selects. Those who do not succeed in this analysis will either suffer the distress of having nothing worthwhile to do or of being constantly overtaxed by excessive activity.

The Nobel Prize laureate Albert Szent-Györgyi expressed this thought very elegantly:

Human activity is dominated by the search for happiness. Happiness, in its turn is, essentially, self-fulfillment, a state in which all needs, be they material or intellectual, are satisfied. Pleasure is the satisfaction of a need and there can be no great pleasure without a great need. Ability brings with it the need to use that ability.

*The effects of stress may be long-lasting, even af-
ter the stressor has ceased to act.* On the bodily
level, we know of many specific immune reactions which can offer long-term protection after a
single exposure to a bacterium or a snake venom.
But there is also a nonspecific resistance that can
be acquired by making continuous but moderate
demands upon our organs, for example, our muscles and brain. Here, the lasting gain is to keep
them fit, the lasting loss is caused by overexertion,
resulting in irreparable tissue breakdown.

In interpersonal stress, the gain is the incitement
in others of friendship, gratitude, goodwill, and
love toward ourselves; the loss is the creation in
others of hatred, frustration, and an urge for revenge. This applies both to people around us and
to ourselves, for our own positive or negative feelings toward others respectively benefit or hurt us
directly, just as much as we are helped or hurt by
inciting those feelings in others.

The most important lasting after-effects of the
way we cope with the demands of interpersonal
relations are too complicated to be explicable in
biochemical terms today, although even this may
eventually become possible. They are essentially
based on memories of previous experiences—pre-
judgments of probable future behavior as far as
one can predict it from the past. The word
"prejudice" has lost its original meaning and in

present-day usage has a deservedly bad connotation as an opinion based not on experience but on ignorance. But, actually, all the wisdom derived from experience is "prejudice" in its obsolete sense: the trained expert can make more reasonable predictions in planning for the future by taking into account what he has learned from the outcome of comparable earlier events. Such events may have created three types of feelings or attitudes: positive, negative, and indifferent.

1. *Positive feelings* can be described as "love" in its broadest sense, as we have defined it at the outset. This includes gratitude, respect, trust, and admiration for the excellence of outstanding achievements, all of which add up to goodwill and friendship. If we think of love in this general sense, collecting it can become the ultimate aim in life because, as far as science can determine, this ultimate aim is the maintenance and enjoyment of life itself. Our homeostatic security in society is best ensured by the incitement of positive feelings toward us in as many people as possible, for no one would have any personal motive in attacking someone whom he loves, respects, and trusts, to whom he feels grateful, or whose excellence in some field demonstrates the feasibility of achievements which may be worth duplicating.

2. *Negative feelings* include hatred, distrust, disdain, hostility, jealousy, and the urge for revenge;

in short, every drive likely to endanger your security by inciting aggressiveness in others who are afraid that you may cause them harm.

3. *Feelings of indifference* at best can lead to an attitude of tolerance. They may make peaceful coexistence possible, but no more.

In the final analysis, incitement of these three types of feelings is the most important factor governing behavior in everyday life. Such feelings are chiefly responsible for our anxieties or peace of mind, our sense of security or insecurity, of fulfillment or frustration; in short, they determine whether we can make a success of life by enjoying its challenging stress without suffering distress.

We must fully understand that these positive, negative, and indifferent attitudes are built into the very substance of living matter. They regulate homeostatic adaptation on all levels of interaction, between cell and cell, man and man, nation and nation. If we truly understand and fully accept this, we will be better prepared to direct that part of our behavior that is, or can be brought, under voluntary control. This includes virtually every decision concerning attitudes among members of a family, a team of coworkers, or even a group of nations.

The imperative biological laws of cybernetic self-defense make it difficult to earn love by constantly choosing purely altruistic decisions. However, it is easy to pursue the altruistic egotism which admittedly tries to help others for the selfish motive of deserving their help in return.

It is also difficult to suppress the impulse for revenge when we are unjustly attacked, because it stems from the natural wish to teach others that it does not pay to hurt us. When we punish a mischievous child, we unwillingly come very close to revenge even if we are guided by parental love. Punishment attempts to condition proper future conduct by the fear of retaliation. Unfortunately, it is often hard to draw the line between constructive teaching by punishment and senseless, purely vindictive retaliation or the desire for self-assertion. Professional teachers and even members of a family are not always very adept at making this distinction. Yet, to follow our code of conduct, we must learn to see the difference very clearly. All our interpersonal relations in everyday life should be guided by the desire to help through the establishment of useful feedback systems by conditioned reflexes, which show what is likely to bring reward or punishment respectively. However, we must avoid even the mildest forms of senseless vendetta, inspired by blind hatred, which only incites even more cruel retaliation.

*The synergy of teamwork.* The advantage of cooperation among animal and human societies has already been mentioned. There is the further significance in teamwork—involving commitment and communal responsibilities—that, whenever feats of extraordinary endurance are required, the inspiration of a common ideal or purpose is the best way to help each individual to endure hardships. The splendid performance of the population of London during the Blitz and of the Russians in the Siege of Leningrad demonstrates the persistence and courage that can be thus inspired. These were impressive instances of psychosocial heterostasis in meeting extraordinary demands for the maintenance of resistance to overwhelming distress. Moreover, a common purpose inspires not only physical endurance and fortitude but even mental feats; for example, microbiologists agree that the extraordinarily rapid development of penicillin was possible only because groups of scientists in many countries were impelled to rise above all questions of national pride or personal scientific credit and pool their efforts to make this efficient antibiotic available for wounded soldiers in the field.

*Frustration.* How is it that the same work can create stress or distress? Nothing breeds success more than success, nothing blocks it more than frustration. Even the greatest experts in the field do not know why the stress of frustration is so much more likely than that of excessive muscular work to produce disease (peptic ulcers, migraine, high blood pressure, or even a simple "pain in the neck"). In fact, physical exercise can even relax and help us withstand mental frustration.

The only explanation we have to offer is the one given in the section "What Is Stress?" in which I tried to illustrate how the same reaction can produce different lesions. Since stress is defined as the consequence of any demand made upon the body, it is difficult to understand, at first sight, why one stressor would act quite differently from another. But, as we have seen, this is presumably because the nonspecific stressor effects are always complicated by the specific effects of the stressor itself, and also by inherited or acquired predispositions which can greatly modify the manifestations of stress. Certain emotional factors, such as frustration, are particularly likely to turn stress into distress, whereas in most instances, physical exercise has an opposite effect. But even here there are exceptions. For example, in a coronary candidate, physical exertion can undoubtedly provoke a cardiac accident.

I would say that, among people engaged in the most common occupations of modern society—the lower and middle echelons of business, industry, agriculture, and public life, from the simple handyman to the administrator or public servant with limited responsibilities—one of the major sources of distress arises from dissatisfaction with life, namely, from disrespect for their own accomplishments. As they grow older and progress towards the completion of their career, they tend to doubt the importance of their achievements. They are frustrated by the conviction that they really could have done, and would have liked to do, much more. These people often spend the rest of their lives in search of scapegoats, grumbling about the lack of opportunity, excessive responsibilities towards their relatives—anything will do to avoid the most painful confession: that the fault was really their own. Could such people get some guidance from a better understanding of the biological laws that govern homeostasis through the stress mechanism?

I think it is worth trying.

Some light can be thrown on the problem by remembering what was said earlier about our adaptation energy appearing to be a hereditarily determined, fixed amount of vitality that must necessarily be spent for man to satisfy his innate urge for self-expression—to complete whatever he considers his mission, whatever tasks he feels he has been built to perform.

This rule again is not merely born out of man's imagination or some artificially rationalized code; it is the manifestation of a deep-rooted natural law, presumably related to the cyclicity of biological phenomena. Countless are the instances in Nature of phenomena which must run in cycles, such as seasonal and diurnal variations in various metabolic reactions, the periodically recurring need for food, water, sleep, sexual activity. Extensive technical studies have dealt with the intimate mechanisms of each of these cycles. But for our purpose, suffice it to say that essentially they are due to the periodic accumulation or exhaustion of chemical materials in the course of normal life. Hence, damage is unavoidable unless each cycle is allowed to run its full course: the accumulating excess of waste products must be eliminated, the undue depletion of indispensable ingredients compensated.

The biological necessity for cyclical completion applies also to controllable human behavior. Blocking the fulfillment of man's natural drives causes as much distress as the forced prolongation and intensification of any activity beyond the desired level. Ignoring this rule leads to frustration, fatigue, and exhaustion which can progress to a mental or physical breakdown.

However, the body is not built to take too much stress always on the same part. In stress research, we have found that, when completion of one particular task becomes impossible, diversion, a voluntary change of activity, is frequently as good as—

if not better than—a rest. For example, when either
fatigue or enforced interruption prevents us from
finishing a mathematical problem, it is better to go
for a swim than just to sit around.

The noted American psychologist William
James illustrates the utility of diversion by an
example which all of us must have experienced at
one time or another:

> You know how it is when you try to rec-
> ollect a forgotten name. Usually you help
> the recall by working for it, but sometimes
> the effort fails . . . and then the opposite ex-
> pedient succeeds. Give up the effort entire-
> ly: think of something different, and in
> half an hour the lost name comes saunter-
> ing into your mind, as Emerson says, as
> carelessly as if it had never been invited.

Substituting demands upon our musculature for
those previously made upon the intellect not only
gives our brain a rest but helps us to avoid worry-
ing about the frustrating interruption. In other
words, stress on one system helps to relax another.
Actually, when completion becomes temporarily
impossible, a diversion into a substitute activity
only simulates completion, but it does so quite
efficiently and usually provides its own satisfac-

tion. We shall have more to say about this in the next section, "Work and Leisure."

To me, the most interesting aspect of the innate requirements for cyclicity is its relation to the three phases of the G.A.S., which it reproduces in miniature form as many as several times a day and, in its full course, throughout a life span. Whatever demand is made upon us, we proceed through (1) the initial alarm reaction of surprise and anxiety because of our inexperience in dealing with a new situation; (2) the stage of resistance when we have learned to cope with the task efficiently and without undue commotion; (3) the stage of exhaustion, a depletion of our energy reserves which leads to fatigue. As I mentioned in Chapter 1, these three stages, which repeat themselves throughout life whenever we are faced with a demand, are surprisingly similar to the lability of inexperienced childhood, the stable resistance of adulthood, and the final exhaustion of senility and death.

In formulating a natural code of behavior, these thoughts are of fundamental importance. We must not only understand the deep-rooted biological need for the completion and fulfillment of our aspirations, but we must also know how to handle these in harmony with our particular inherited capacities. Not everybody is born with the same amount of adaptation energy.

## WORK AND LEISURE

As Montaigne said, "Fame and tranquility can never be bedfellows." It is the hunger for achievement that brings *joie de vivre*. You must be very hungry to really enjoy a meal. You must really want to win to be totally mobilized for a fight. That is why great peaks of accomplishment were achieved by the gladiators and toreadors who had to fight or die, by the saints who gladly endured torture and even death to please God, and by the patriots who considered it an honor to die for king or country.

Deprivation of motivation is the greatest mental tragedy because it destroys all guidelines. The man who knows he suffers from an incurable disease and has nothing left to work for, the billionaire to whom any further accumulation of wealth would be meaningless, the truly blasé person or "congenital pensioner" who finds no satisfaction in rising above the minimum level needed for comparatively painless survival, are all equally unhappy.

I am not going to tell you what should motivate you; whether you wish to serve God, king, country, family, political party, to work for good causes, or to fulfill your "duty" is up to you. I only want to show that motivation—preferably an ambition to accomplish something that really satisfies you and hurts no one—is essential. It seems to me that a way of life based on the understanding of man's responses to stress and to constant change is the only way that leads out of the present jungle of conflicting judgments about right and wrong, justice and injustice, in which our sense of values has become entangled and obscured.

The many technological innovations and the social changes in family structure, in the respective rights and duties of men and women, and in the type of work now in demand because of urbanization which I have witnessed during my own lifetime have faced society with unprecedented requirements for constant adaptability. Those of us who have experienced all these transitions cannot stand by idly, watching the gradual displacement in the young of a sense of purpose by a sense of despair.

To overcome the present wave of unnerving frustration that can express itself only in violence and brutality, young people must be convinced that they cannot succeed in quenching their normal thirst for achievement by the compulsive hunt for more and more amorous victories or by trying to attract attention through bizarre behavior. There is no way to escape the reality they cannot face—least of all by blunting their vision of it with the short-lived pleasure offered by drugs.

They need help so that they may learn from their predecessors what techniques of adaptation and readaptation are helpful or harmful. Adaptation, like stress, is a problem in itself, irrespective of the circumstances to which we must adapt or the agents that cause stress. These general laws can be taught, if not through structured scholarly courses, at least through apprenticeship, by giving an example, or through the very human technique of talking things over and trying to bridge the generation gap with warmth and mutual trust.

Nor are the problems related to the need for constant readaptation to sudden social and technological changes limited to youth. They affect large sections of contemporary society throughout the world.

*Man must work.* I think we have to begin by clearly realizing that work is a biological necessity. Just as our muscles become flabby and degenerate if not used, so our brain slips into chaos and confusion unless we constantly use it for some work that seems worthwhile to us. The average person thinks he works for economic security or social status, but when, at the end of a most successful business career, he has finally achieved this, there remains nothing to fight for—no hope for progress, only the boredom of assured monotony.

The great Canadian physician William Osler recognized the significance of work in this tribute:

> Though little, the master word looms large in meaning. It is the "open sesame" to every portal, the great equalizer, the philosopher's stone which transmutes all base metal of humanity into gold. The stupid it will make bright, the bright brilliant, and the brilliant steady. To youth, it brings hope, to the middle-aged confidence, to the aged repose. It is directly responsible for all advances in medicine during the past twenty-five years. Not only has it been the touchstone of progress, but it is the measure of success in everyday life. And the master word is WORK.

Do not listen to the tempting slogans of those who keep repeating, "There is more to life than just work," or, "You should work to live, not live to work." This sounds pretty convincing, but is it really? Of course, these statements are true in themselves, yet your principal aim should be not to avoid work but to find the kind of occupation which, for you, is play. The best way to avoid harmful stress is to select an environment (wife, boss, friends) which is in line with your innate preferences—to find an activity which you like and respect. Only thus can you eliminate the need for frustrating constant readaptation that is the major cause of distress.

*Stress is the spice of life.* Since stress is associated with all types of activity, we could avoid most of it only by never doing anything. Who would enjoy a life of no runs, no hits, no errors? Besides—as we have said earlier—certain types of activities have a curative effect and actually help to keep the stress mechanism in good shape.

It is well known that occupational therapy is one of the most efficient ways of dealing with certain mental diseases, and that exercise of your muscles keeps you fit. It all depends on the type of work you do and the way you react to it.

The continuous leisure of enforced retirement or of solitary confinement—even if the food and bed were the best in the world—is certainly not an attractive way of life. In medicine, it is now a generally accepted principle not to enforce complete bed rest for long even after an operation.

On the endless journeys of the old sailing ships, when there was often nothing to do for weeks, the sailors had to be kept busy—washing the desk or painting the boat—or mutiny would have been the one relief from boredom. The same considerations of stressful boredom apply to crews on long voyages in nuclear submarines, to scientists spending the winter in Antarctica, immobilized for months by the weather, and of course even more to the astronauts who will have to face loneliness and sensory deprivation for extremely long periods. During the fuel shortage and labor strikes, the three-day work week in England upset family life by driving workers to the pubs for "leisure."

In fact, for many older people (even the avowed egotists), the most difficult aspect of retirement to bear is the feeling of being useless. It is not for themselves that they want to work; they realize only too well that the end is near and that they cannot take their earnings with them beyond the grave. As Benjamin Franklin aptly said: "There is nothing wrong with retirement as long as one doesn't allow it to interfere with one's work."

*What is work and what is leisure?* According to George Bernard Shaw's aphorism: "Labor is doing what we must; leisure is doing what we like." Even reading the best prose or poetry is work for the professional literary critic, as tennis or golf is work for the paid pro. Yet the athlete may read for relaxation, and the man of letters may engage in sports for his change of pace. The rich executive, though he would not think of relaxing by moving his heavy furniture, will enjoy his regular workout in the gym of his expensive club. Fishing, gardening, or almost any other occupation is work when you have to do it for a living, play if you choose to do it for fun.

Bertrand Russell obviously liked walking, even though he called it labor:

> Our mental make-up is suited to a life of very severe physical labor. I used, when I was younger, to take my holidays walking. I would cover twenty-five miles a day, and when evening came, I had no need of anything to keep me from boredom, since the delight of sitting amply sufficed.

As I have said, work is a basic need of man. The question is not whether we should or should not work, but what kind of work suits us best. To function normally, man needs work as he needs air, food, sleep, social contacts, and sex. Few people would enthusiastically welcome the day of test-tube babies, making sex superfluous for procreation; let us not look forward with eager anticipation to the time when technology will take over such activities.

The Western world is being racked by the insatiable demand for less work and more pay. To achieve this is not enough. Stress is associated with every kind of work, but distress is not. We must ask ourselves: Less work to get more time for what? More pay to buy what? Few people give much thought to what they will do with their free time and extra money after they have achieved a comfortable assured income. Of course, there is such a thing as a living wage; inflation has become a threat not only to the poor, but even to fairly affluent people. In practice, the urgency of the clamor for improvement does not depend so much upon the number of working hours or the salaries earned as upon the degree of dissatisfaction with life. We could do much—and at little cost—by fighting this dissatisfaction.

Why should we work so hard to avoid work? The French philosopher Henri Bergson justly pointed out that it would be more appropriate to call our species *Homo faber* (the making man) than *Homo sapiens* (the knowing man), for the characteristic feature of man is not his wisdom but his constant urge to work on improving his environment and himself. The leisure fans would like to call us *Homo ludens* (the playing man), but the desire to play without a goal is not a distinguishing human trait; we share it with kittens, puppies, and most other animals. Neither, of course, is the drive to build limited to our species; beavers, bees, and ants are great architects of complex structures. All this illustrates again how generally applicable the great laws of Nature are, since the drive to work and construct is one of them.

Your most important aim should not be to work as little as possible while earning enough to acquire the security that you will never have to work much harder. For the full enjoyment of leisure, you have to be tired first, as for the full enjoyment of food the best cook is hunger.

Only the sick or mentally handicapped really prefer not to work. Short hours are a boon only for those who cannot find occupations that interest them. Admittedly, it is difficult to get much satisfaction out of being a garbage collector, night watchman, or executioner, and those who can earn their livelihood in no other way are justified in striving for "less work and more pay," and seeking other outlets for self-fulfillment in their spare time. But, fortunately, not many occupations fall into this category. Many more people suffer because they have no particular taste for anything, no hunger for achievement. These—not those who earn little—are the true paupers of mankind. What they need more than money is guidance.

Those who can afford to retire and do not want to are probably fortunate enough to have found the type of work which fulfills their need for achievement.

*Social implications.* We have already touched upon the utility of interpersonal and social altruistic egotism. With the progress of science and automation, most of the tedious, unpleasant activities will no longer be necessary, and more people will have to worry about what to do with their leisure time. Soon we will be able to cut down on obligatory working hours to a point where work deprivation will become our major problem. If man has no more incentive to work out his role as *Homo faber*, he is likely to seek destructive, revolutionary outlets to relieve his basic need for self-assertive activity. He may be able to solve his age-old problem of having to live by the sweat of his brow, but the fatal enemy of all utopias is boredom. What we shall have to do after technology makes most "useful work" redundant is to invent new occupations.

Nothing to do is not to rest; a vacant mind and a slothful body suffer the distress of deprivation.

Let us start preparing right now not only to fight pollution and the population explosion, but also to combat boredom when lack of work threatens to become extremely dangerous. It will require a full-scale effort to teach "play professions"—the arts, philosophy, crafts, science—to the public at large; there is no limit to how much man can work on the perfection of his own self.

Incidentally, in discussing these views at lectures, I have repeatedly met with critics who asserted that completely unproductive play is as justified as work. As I have said earlier in this book, I do not intend to make moral judgments about anyone's life style that is not harmful to other people. However, as a biologist, I must point out that, while totally unproductive play (solving crossword puzzles, collecting matchboxes, training a parrot to speak) has its justification as a form of mental or physical exercise and as a diversion after work, it is not likely to earn much goodwill or security in society. Most people who engage in these activities could get just as much pleasure and satisfaction from more productive play, even if only by striving for the stimulating example of championship, of excellence in sports or feats of endurance. Play can also serve to earn goodwill by preparing the mind and body for more generally useful accomplishments, just as the make-believe games of children prepare them for the development of skills in adult life, in the same way as finger exercises adapt the hands of the pianist for future creative achievements. But pure play merely for self-indulgence is certainly not a long-range aim likely to ensure your homeostasis or even a satisfactory feeling of accomplishment.

I have tried to sketch the way I see the relationship between stress, work, and leisure. Perhaps this outline could serve as a basis for planning a better, healthier philosophy than that which guides our society now. I think we should adapt our moral code and values to fit the exigencies of the times to come. But I do not feel competent to preach what I have learned. Besides, it would be contrary to my basic predilection for professionalism—for sticking to what we can do well. I have been trained to do medical research. Laboratory work on stress can furnish a solid scientific basis for social improvements. But what will be needed are sociologists, philosophers, psychologists, economists, and statesmen, who can prepare the territory by readjusting the motivation of the general public. Then, the communications media must attempt to drive the lesson home and, finally, practical politicians will have to translate the fruits of medical research and psychological reorientation into the terms of a national or even international policy. Meanwhile, it is a dream, but you must first be able to dream before you can even try to make your dream come true. The conquest of smallpox, the invention of television, a trip to the moon, were all but dreams before they became realities.

No society can be entirely just; ours is certainly not. Unfortunately, there are two types of influential people, and their methods and aims are often at odds.

There are those of us who like to produce, to create, primarily for the love of creation, but also because any good thing—a symphony, an industry, or a well-painted wall—earns goodwill, gratitude, and recognition. The producers are busy producing; they have not much time or taste for anything else.

Then, there are the schemers and plotters who work for influence and power; some of these are vicious and ruthless, others are well-meaning idealists. But even for the idealists, retaining their influence, staying in power, must be the first aim; for what is the use of the best ideas if they cannot be put into action? It is these men who write and preach our code of ethics, and, to a large extent, even make our laws. They also hold the purse strings. Unfortunately, the talents for spiritual guidance and those for staying in power do not always run together.

You may ask: If the producers are so ingenious, creative, and dedicated to progress, couldn't they beat the unproductive plotters at their own game? In theory, yes, but not in practice. Eminent producers usually have greater intellectual gifts than the clever schemers, but they could not use them for this kind of activity because they are repulsed by it; and, if they overcome their aversion, their creativity would soon wither. The two types of activities are not easily compatible.

*My rose garden.* Meanwhile, I try to console my young assistants by telling them that perhaps those of us who collect love and goodwill don't need money as much as some other people because much of what we might want to buy is given to us free. I remember having spent an evening at the luxurious home of a physician who has built up an extremely lucrative private practice in California. After dinner, we sat before the enormous scenic window of his living room and looked out into the darkness. He explained that he is fond of flowers, and that outside the window is a rose garden—which he then proceeded to illuminate in red, green, blue, and every other shade of the spectrum by pressing different buttons on a control panel attached to his armchair. It was a rather expensive and complex installation often in need of repair, he said, but after a tiresome day in the office he liked to relax by contemplating this display.

I also am fond of flowers, and at first I thought with self-pity about how far I was from being able to afford anything like this. The single cactus I own looks very plain by comparison. But then I wouldn't really enjoy Nature by pressing the buttons on that panel; after a few minutes, I am afraid, I would get bored. My "rose garden" is the Institute of Experimental Medicine and Surgery. It permits me to contemplate much more wondrous and varied aspects of Nature. In addition, it occasionally turns up a useful fruit. Besides—come to think of it—I can even brag that my playground is much more expensive than his and I don't have to pay for it from taxable income; it is given to me free and I am paid to play in it.

*Stress and aging.* There exists a close relationship between work, stress, and aging. Stress, as I have said, is the nonspecific response to any kind of demand at any one time; aging results from the sum of all the stresses to which the body has been exposed during a lifetime and apparently corresponds to the "stage of exhaustion" of the G.A.S., which is, in a sense, an accelerated version of normal aging. Under the influence of intense stress, the alarm reaction, the stage of resistance, and the stage of exhaustion are evoked in rapid succession. The main difference between aging and the G.A.S. appears to be that the latter is more or less reversible under the influence of rest. But we must keep in mind that as long as man lives he is always under some measure of stress, and that, although stress and aging may be closely related, they are definitely not identical.

A newborn baby, while crying and struggling, is under considerable stress—in fact, distress—but shows no sign of aging, whereas a man of ninety, quietly sleeping in his bed, is under no great stress but shows all the signs of aging.

Each period of stress, especially if it results from frustrating, unsuccessful struggles, leaves some irreversible chemical scars which accumulate to constitute the signs of tissue aging. Many authors still use my earlier definition of biological stress as "the wear and tear" in the machinery of a living being, but this is actually the *result* of stress, and the accumulation of the irreparable part of this attrition is aging.

As I mentioned in Chapter 1, we have no objective way of measuring adaptability at any given moment; but there appears to be a superficial, readily available, replaceable type, and another more deeply hidden in reserves which can replenish the superficial kind only after some rest or diversion of activity. These could be viewed as requirements for working two types of sewage-disposal systems. In biochemical terms, we might think of exhaustion as largely due to accumulating undesirable by-products of vital chemical reactions. Much of our metabolic debris is readily eliminated, thus reestablishing the original equilibrium. But a small fraction of the countless chemical processes needed for adaptation to the demands made upon us by life results in insoluble waste products that clog up the machinery of the body until it is no longer usable.

The so-called "aging pigments" which accumulate in the cells (especially in those of the heart and liver) of very old people are microscopically visible insoluable precipitates of this kind. Heavy calcium deposits in arteries, joints, and the crystalline lens of the eye are other by-products that illustrate this interpretation of aging. In fact, we have used a technique for the production of calcium deposits to induce a kind of premature senility in animals.

The diminishing elasticity of connective tissue is also probably due to the formation of stable waste products in which macromolecules of protein are fixed by cross-linkages between them. Such processes (excessive proliferation of rigid connective tissue and deposits of insoluble foreign materials, e.g., calcium, cholesterol) largely account for the progressive hardening of aging blood vessels. As these lose their elasticity, the blood pressure must rise to maintain circulation through them, despite their stiffness and narrowing. The resulting hypertension, in turn, causes a predisposition to cardiovascular accidents, particularly strokes.

Another mechanism that leads to the final exhaustion of adaptibility during senility is the cumulative effect of continuously losing small bits of irreplaceable tissue (in the brain, heart, etc.), usually owing to injuries or minor vascular ruptures. In the young, these defects are readily compensated by the ample supply of remaining healthy tissue, but in the course of a long life, our tissue reserves are all used up. In the aged, these losses are replaced by actual connective scar tissues. They are added to the "chemical scars" of the piled-up metabolic debris which—as previously mentioned— cannot be eliminated.

But successful activity, no matter how intense, leaves you with comparatively few such scars; it causes stress but little, if any, distress. On the contrary, it provides you with the exhilarating feeling of youthful strength, even at a very advanced age. Work wears you out mainly through the frustration of failure. Many of the most eminent among the hard workers in almost any field lived a long life. They overcame their inevitable frustrations by the great preponderance of success. Think of Pablo Casals, Winston Churchill, Haile Selassie, Albert Schweitzer, G. B. Shaw, Henry Ford, Charles de Gaulle, Bertrand Russell, Queen Victoria, Titian, Voltaire, Bismarck, Michaelangelo, Pablo Picasso, Henri Matisse, Arthur Rubinstein, Arturo Toscanini and—in my own profession of medical research—the Nobel Prize winners Sir Henry Dale, Pavlov, Albert Szent-Györgyi, Otto Loewi, Selman Waksman, Otto Warburg. All these people continued to be successful—and, what is more important, on the whole happy—well into their seventies, eighties, or even late nineties. Of course, none of them ever "worked" at all, in the sense of work as something one has to do to earn a living but does not enjoy. Despite their many years of intense activity, they lived a life of constant leisure by always doing what they liked to do.

It is true that few people belong to this category of the creative elite; admittedly, their success in meeting the challenge of stress cannot serve as a basis for a general code of behavior. But you can live long and happily by working hard along more modest lines if you have found the proper job and are reasonably successful at it.

When I entered medical school at the age of eighteen, I was so fascinated by the possibilities of research on life and disease that I used to get up at four o'clock in the morning to study in our garden until about six in the evening, with very few interruptions. My mother knew nothing about biological stress, but I still remember her telling me that this sort of thing could not be kept up for more than a couple of months and would undoubtedly precipitate a nervous breakdown. Now, at the age of sixty-seven, I still get up at four or five o'clock in the morning and still work until six at night, with few interruptions; and I am still perfectly happy leading this kind of life. No regrets. To combat the physical decay of senility, my only concession so far has been to set aside an hour a day to keep my muscles trim by swimming or by racing around the McGill campus on a bicycle at five in the morning.

The philosophy of work to earn goodwill is

applicable to almost any occupation. A carpenter can have a sense of satisfaction and pride while displaying his well-made table; a tailor or a shoemaker can get pleasure and the feeling of fulfillment from his own craftsmanship in making an admirable suit or pair of shoes. Unfortunately, most of these professions have become more or less obsolete as a result of the efficiency of modern machinery. Nevertheless, recognition that the boredom of working on an assembly line causes absenteeism is gradually forcing management to modify this form of mass production. Despite its extraordinary practical advantages, the assembly line cannot satisfy the worker's natural desire for an identifiably personal accomplishment. New production methods are now being explored that offer incentives for teamwork, with groups of workers jointly taking responsibility for separate aspects of the manufacturing process.

However, there will still remain many tasks which require no particular craft or artistic talent and yet offer the satisfaction of a job well done. Whenever I take a taxi, I like to converse with the drivers, many of whom tell me that they like their jobs, despite the frustrations of traffic tie-ups. Some of the older ones claim that they could afford to retire but prefer to do something useful, especially because they enjoy talking to their customers; and they get pleasure from earning a grateful smile for having been efficient and courteous. (No. I am quite sure it is not always only the tip that counts.)

Pride in excellence is again a primeval biological feeling; it is not limited to our species. Even a hunting dog is proud to bring in his quarry unscathed; just look at his face and you will see that his work has made him happy. A performing seal is manifestly pleased by earning applause. Only the stress of frustration, of lack of purpose, can spoil the satisfaction of performance. Friction and constant aimless changes in direction are as prone to cause wear and tear and the accumulation of wastes in living machines as in inanimate ones.

The art is to find, among the jobs you are capable of doing, the one you really like best—and that people appreciate. Man must have recognition; he cannot tolerate constant censure, for that is what—more than any other stressor—makes work frustrating and harmful.

*What is duty?* You often hear impressive remarks —usually propounded in a doctrinal tone that admits no contradiction—about the importance of fulfilling your "duty." Only a few days ago, my eighteen-year-old son André got an assignment in school to write an essay about his duties.

Bewildering.

What are his duties? Who has the authority to

impose them upon him? The church, parents, society?

To my mind, duty is a self-imposed code of conduct. Its main purpose is to stabilize our course of action in life by a given set of standards which we respect and which we think will be respected by others. We must be convinced that by following this code we shall earn not only the feeling of fulfillment but also, if possible, the goodwill of our neighbors.

Duty so defined immediately raises the question of who is the neighbor toward whom I should acknowledge duties. You cannot earn the goodwill and love of all your neighbors by any particular types of activities; besides, interests differ and may even clash. Some are most interested in large but unselected populations (all of humanity, the poor, the old, the handicapped); others try to serve a select few by the creation of culture, art, philosophy; yet others accept as their principal motivation service to family, country, church, a political party, science, medicine. The choice is a matter of taste, and tastes cannot be judged by reason. If somebody is not doing what you like (for example, if a student is spending too much time on things other than his studies, or an investigator on activities unrelated to science), do not blame him. Remember that he could blame you with equal justification for your devoting too much time to your preferred topic.

Many of those who spend much time on things other than their "official" duty or occupation often feel righteous about their secondary endeavors. They consider it their obligation to devote time to "civic duties" or to live a "cultural life," dismissing as single-minded those who give all their time to one particular activity that they do not appreciate or do not understand. Remember that this also is a matter of taste, and everyone has a right to concentrate or spread his efforts as he wishes. It is self-deceit to elevate any "extracurricular" activity sanctimoniously into an obligation instead of confessing that we do it just because we like it. And, indeed, as G. B. Shaw put it: "When a stupid man is doing something he is ashamed of, he always declares that it is his duty." However, this is not necessarily so; as Friedrich Nietzsche says in a more poetic tone:

I slept and I dreamed that life is pleasure;
I woke and I saw that life is duty;
I worked and I notice that duty is pleasure.

# 3

# What is the aim of life?

An AIM is a "direction or guidance as to a course or procedure to be followed . . . the object intended to be attained." Synonyms: "Purpose, design. . . ."

A GOAL is "the end toward which effort or ambition is directed."

—*Webster's Third New International Dictionary*

I shall try to deal with this problem purely as a biologist in the light of my laboratory experience. In this context, "aim" may appear to be a presumptuous word; ascribing a purpose to physiological processes observed in the laboratory would seem even more so. Teleology, the concept of an inherent design in Nature, is based on the assumption that Nature herself, like man, prefers one thing to happen instead of another, just as you or I may wish our own family to prosper rather than that of a stranger. Scientifically, this would be difficult to prove. What I mean here is merely that life must be allowed to run its natural course toward the fulfillment of its innate potential. To a biologist, this represents a pretty fair equivalent of what men of God, sages, and philosophers would call *the* aim of life.

In this sense, and to my mind, the aim of life is to maintain its own identity and express its innate abilities and drives with the least possible frustration. To remain healthy, man must have some goal, some purpose in life that he can respect and be proud to work for. Each person must work out a way to relieve his pent-up energy without creating conflicts with his fellow men and, if possible, to earn their goodwill and respect.

## AIMS AND MEANS

To start with, a clear distinction must be made between our final aims—the ultimate achievements that give purpose to life—and the means through which we hope to attain them. For example, money is never a final aim; it has no value in itself. It can only act as a means, helping us to reach some ultimate goal which, to us, has inherent value. Few people think about the fundamental difference between aims and means, but without clearly recognizing this difference, you cannot achieve peace of mind. Means are good only to reach some final accomplishment which deep in our soul we can truly respect. In well-balanced, happy people this is almost always the urge for self-expression and the desire to earn the love and esteem of their neighbors.

The only philosophy in which ultimate aims and means virtually coincide is the purely hedonistic way of life; it disregards all aims except those that give immediate personal gratification (e.g., the pleasures of the gourmet, the passive enjoyment of art, travel, nature). No value judgment is implied here, only a distinction between introverted and extroverted means of obtaining one's own aims. Whether we admire, share, or are indifferent to the pleasures of the gourmet or the aesthete, in essence, their aims are always purely introverted and self-centered, whereby they differ from the pleasures of the superb chef, musician, or sculptor who craves to be creative and wishes to earn the goodwill of his neighbor by giving him something.

*Short-term goals.* Our short-term goals provide immediate gratification. They have nothing to do with our satisfaction in the distant future; rewards of this type cannot be stored, they do not add up to an ever-growing reserve of strength or happiness. The only traces they may leave are those of pleasant memories.

Most of these short-term objectives aim at pleasure now: the gratification of sensual desires, the solving of a complicated crossword puzzle, the taste of good food or wine, a drive through beautiful countryside. In all these instances, you derive satisfaction by merely doing what you like to do, without any further reward in mind that might help you or others in the future. Most of these short-term objectives require no particular training, although some of the more sophisticated among them presuppose a carefully developed, acquired taste. Anybody can enjoy an excellent meal, but the trained palate of the gourmet can get more pleasure out of it. You also need special grooming to appreciate the fine points of great music, painting, or sculpture; you need a whole life of study to get the full benefits of understanding complex scientific subjects. Thus, not all the rewards of short-term objectives are enjoyed in a purely passive manner; you must seek them out, driven by the need for self-expression as, for instance, through creative activities and various games. Yet, here, action and reward are virtually simultaneous and short-lived.

*Long-term goals.* The search for a satisfactory philosophy of life must begin with self-analysis. We have to answer for ourselves as honestly as we can: What do we really want from life? As in all biological classifications, the categories overlap. We usually have two or more long-range aims, of which one is almost always dominant, and we shall see later that these individually different final aims are all, consciously or unconsciously, designed to earn the love of our neighbors.

To give meaning and direction to life, we need a lofty long-range purpose. That is why our natural ultimate aim must have two salient characteristics: it must be something that requires hard work (otherwise it would give no outlet to self-expression), and its fruits must be sufficiently permanent to accumulate as life goes by (otherwise it could not be a long-range aim). Philosophical, religious, and political ideals have long and effectively served man in his search for a long-term objective to which he can devote his whole life. Even the most ardently desired aim, if it be short-lived, could furnish a motive only for the moment, but a long-range aim offering us permanent directives throughout life can eliminate many of the frustrating doubts that cause distress about the choice of our actions.

Besides, as I have mentioned before, collecting or hoarding is as characteristic of life as is egotism; in fact, it is one of the manifestations of selfishness. Even many primitive animals instinctively hoard things that they may need in the future to ensure their own security. The work of accumulating food or building highly organized living quarters is a basic biological drive. As I have emphasized earlier, it is as characteristic of ants, bees, squirrels, and beavers as of the capitalist who collects money to put away in the bank. The same impulse drives entire human societies to amass a system of roads, telephones, cities, and fortifications that strike them as useful means of accumulating the ingredients of security and comfort.

In man, this urge first manifests itself when children start to amass matchboxes, shells, or stickers; it continues when adults gather stamps or coins. The natural drive for collecting is certainly not an artificial, indoctrinated tradition. By collecting certain things, you acquire status and security in your community. My suggested guideline to earning love merely attempts to direct the hoarding instinct toward what I consider the most permanent and valuable commodity that man can collect: a huge capital of goodwill which protects him against personal attacks by his fellow men.

It must be admitted that most of us go about this in a very inefficient way, which defeats our purpose. Yet, the basic need for earning goodwill and approval is always there.

Instincts and emotions set the course of life, but logic, guided by intelligence, is the only way to check that you are employing the best means to stay on that course. As previously mentioned, you use pure cool logic only to verify how best to direct your life in the service of an emotionally selected aim.

Ideas (scientific, philosophical, literary) also come intuitively without the guidance of logic. They strike us at the most unexpected times—for example, the idea of writing this book occurred to me one night in the bathtub—but unless you take note and articulate them they evaporate, and you cannot later work them out intellectually by logic.

*Conscious aims.* Both short- and long-range goals may be pursued unconsciously to satisfy basic drives or as consciously accepted guidelines to the ultimate aim, the fulfillment of what we consider our purpose. The conscious aims—whether true or imaginary—fall into four main groups, which can be briefly sketched as follows:

*1. Lean on the powerful.* Pleasing *God*. Serving the *Sovereign* (king, queen, prince) who embodies and symbolizes the concept of fatherland or mother country to which we wish to be loyal. Serving one's *country*. Loyalty to a *political system*, whatever it may be (fascism, communism, the republic or democracy, the monarchy). Promoting the good of the *family*, through self-sacrifice for spouse and children. "May they have what we didn't (or be able to do what we couldn't)." Unswerving adherence to a *code of honor*. These codes differ widely, and are often conflicting, in various cultures. A traditional English gentleman, a religious fanatic or saint, a member of the Mafia, feel obliged to do very different things out of loyalty to their particular code.

*2. Be powerful. Power* for its own sake. *Fame*, the applause of the masses, the acquisition of generally accepted status symbols. *Security*, often sought through acquisition of power. This urge usually becomes dominant because of a great, and often morbid, feeling of insecurity.

*3. Give joy.* Unselfish *philanthropy*, the gifts of *artistic or scientific creations, child care, kindness to animals*, the physician's *urge to cure*, in short, the wish to help others without ulterior motives. Giving a million dollars to charity or a few peanuts to a monkey in the zoo.

*4. Get joy.* All the foregoing are specific, though often overlapping and only seemingly final, motivations, for achieving joy through gratification. But there remains the person who has never thought, or does not care, about any of the above guiding motives: the real *hedonist* who merely seeks self-gratification, no matter through what means. He just lives from day to day, doing whatever gives him the greatest pleasure at the time, no matter how it is obtained, through sex, food, drink, travel, the passive enjoyment of art or a display of power, the desire to have the last word even if he knows he is wrong.

To lean on the powerful or to be powerful are long-range aims; for better or for worse, they can be your guides throughout life. To give joy and get joy offer immediate satisfaction. Although these are all conscious aims, some of them are based much more on tradition and trust in the established value judgments of our society than on natural laws.

*The ultimate commitment.* It seems to me that man's ultimate aim in life is to express himself as fully as possible, according to his own lights, and to achieve a sense of security. To accomplish this, you must first find your optimal stress level, and then use your adaptation energy at a rate and in a direction adjusted to your innate qualifications and preferences.

We have seen that inherited internal conditioning factors are important in determining not only the optimal stress level but also the innate weaknesses in one or the other organ system, thereby predisposing it to break down under intense stress. Of course, everyone should have equal opportunities at birth, but each individual is unique in all aspects of mind and body. Hence, a biologist cannot accept the most commonly quoted and misinterpreted statement in the American Declaration of Independence: "*We hold these truths to be self-evident, that all men are created equal. . . .*"

But whatever goals we strive for, the relationship between stress and the attainment of our aims is so evident that it hardly justifies lengthy discussions. Mental tensions, frustrations, insecurity, and aimlessness are among the most damaging stressors, and psychosomatic studies have shown how often they cause migraine headache, peptic ulcers, heart attacks, hypertension, mental disease, suicide, or just hopeless unhappiness.

In any event, neither short- nor long-range aims are truly the ultimate aim of man, that which should act as a beacon, a guideline for all our actions. I feel we should always strive for what we ourselves—not the society that surrounds us—regard as worthwhile. But we must, at all cost, avoid frustration, the humiliation of failure; we must not aim too high and undertake tasks which are beyond us. Everyone has his own limits. For some of us, these may be near the maximum, for others near the minimum, of what man can attain. But within the limits set by our innate abilities, we should strive for excellence, for the best that we can do. Not for perfection—for that is almost always unattainable—and setting it as an aim can only lead to the distress of frustration. Excellence is a wonderful goal in itself and highly suitable to earn us the goodwill, respect, and even love of our neighbors. Many years ago I put this philosophy into a little jingle. It may sound trivial but, whatever happens during the day to threaten my equanimity or throw some doubt upon the value of my conduct, it helps me to think of these two lines:

> *Fight for your highest attainable aim*
> *But never put up resistance in vain.*

## THE CRAVING FOR APPROVAL AND
### THE DREAD OF CENSURE

Why is everybody so anxious to deny that he is motivated—if not exclusively, at least to a large extent—by the desire for approval and recognition of whatever he does? I have briefly touched upon this problem in discussing the need for acknowledged self-expression.

In principle, as we have seen in Chapter 1, all homeostatic reactions depend upon positive and negative feedback mechanisms in which a demand automatically elicits the corresponding compensatory readjustment. This is equally true of bodily and mental reactions. For example, exposure to cold mobilizes the body's heat-producing apparatus, whereas heat activates responses that help cool us. In everyday life, interpersonal relations are subject to the same type of cybernetic feedback: censure is the natural signal to stop actions which society resents, and conversely, we must rely upon the objective indicators of recognition and approval to assure us that we are on the right track, that our conduct is appreciated. Such feedback provides guidelines for constructive behavior in harmony with our environment.

It only leads to guilt feelings and mental stress for us to be ashamed of and to suppress natural drives that cannot be avoided, especially if they harm no one and may do a great deal of good. There are many things in life that are frowned upon merely because of artificially developed social conventions. For instance, there is no point in announcing to all your guests at a formal party that an urgent biological drive forces you to abandon them for a few moments. But if you gotta go, you gotta go; it is silly to be prudish about it.

So far, I think everybody will agree with me; but it is a singular fact that, among the many great scientists I have met during my long academic career, none would freely admit that public recognition of his achievements (titles, medals, prizes, or other honors) played a decisive role in stimulating his enthusiasm for work. When asked to explain their motivation, curiously, many of them appeared to be quite unprepared for such a question; their first reply was that they never thought much about it. Then, they would usually mention curiosity about the way Nature works, "art for art's own sake," so to speak, or—especially among physicians —the wish to cure. I can say frankly that, as far as I am concerned, the desire for approval and recognition has been one of the major driving forces throughout my life. But most scientists, when pressed to mention additional incentives, will even say that they work for money rather than admit to a desire for public acclaim; after all, "one must live," but one should "never be sensitive to flattery." Perhaps flattery is not the right word to use here. But I will freely admit that I am as proud as a peacock of any recognition and approval that I may have earned. And why shouldn't I be? Whatever I have done—modest as it is in comparison with the immense advances that have been and will be made by many other scientists—I can't help feeling happy about it; just as I am admittedly unhappy that so many of my projects did not come to fruition. I am sure this shameless attitude has saved me a great deal of mental anguish which my more formally ethical colleagues have suffered in the intimacy of their introspection.

I believe it is below the dignity of an objective scientific mind to fool either oneself or others by denying that the desire to earn goodwill and love plays a role in motivation.

This is certainly not to say that the thirst for approval should become the ultimate aim of life. No successful scientist would want a coveted distinction at the price of becoming a petty politician whose energy is consumed by string-pulling to the point where he has no strength left for research.

I have often consoled myself for missed recognitions with an anecdote according to which a friend once said to the distinguished Roman statesman and philosopher, Cato the Elder: "It is a scandal that no statue has been erected to you in Rome! I am going to form a committee."

"No," said Cato, "I would rather have people ask 'Why isn't there a statue to Cato?' than 'Why is there one?'"

Young people can save themselves unnecessary frustration in the course of their careers if they think about these problems unabashed. True, there can be only one captain on a ship, one president of a company, one chairman in a department, but the other members may be just as good or even better. Besides, anyone who must be "the fairest in the land" can, in the intimacy of his own soul, think that he is—even if others do not see him that way. This attitude does him a lot of good and hurts nobody so long as he makes no case of it.

Of course, no discerning person measures his

success by the number of people who acclaim him or by the decibels of their applause. For example, among my colleagues, I am sure that none could enjoy credit for a discovery erroneously attributed to him, and few of them would trade places with the most acclaimed public figure.

Unfortunately, in the life of the average citizen, there are few real highlights or memorable moments from which he can draw satisfaction and pride throughout life—accomplishments that his spiritual "neighbors" would admire and approve as having served a noble aim. In fact, sometimes this urge for approval of ordinary people by their fellow citizens may become quite grotesque.

The little Parisian cobbler who left one of his legs in Russia in the service of Napoleon only to participate in the defeat of the French armies nevertheless remained always grateful to his emperor, who permitted him to taste the nectar of greatness. Without this ingenious chief, he would have spent all his life accumulating the rust of monotony—as the "little cobbler on the corner of Rue des Saints Pères"—since he had no ability of his own to do anything else but earn his bread by repairing old shoes. Even long after his retirement, in chatting with his chums on a bench of the Parc du Luxembourg, he always returned to the summit of his existence, the days when he was a soldier in the Grande Armée, commanded by a great general, fighting for what he considered to be a noble aim.

This story illustrates, better than could a long and learned philosophic discussion, that people of the most different cultural, intellectual, or physical capacities—the domestic worker, artisan, engineer, secretary, poet, philosopher, scientist, or athlete—hunger for peak accomplishment. Whatever our occupation, it gives us great satisfaction and a feeling of fulfillment to accomplish the best and have it recognized—even if only by ourselves.

In discussing a code of behavior, let us add just a word about modesty and immodesty. Truly great men are proud of their work, but, when speaking about it, they will never divert attention from the subject or create confusion about its value by pseudomodest assurances of its unimportance in their own eyes. Nevertheless, they do not boast and for various reasons may not especially wish to discuss the value of their accomplishments.

Besides, as Winston Churchill said about one of his ministers who was known for his extraordinary display of modesty: "Ah yes, but it is easy for him, he has so much to be modest about."

As much as we thirst for approval, we dread condemnation. The common statement "I don't care what people say about me" is just as false as "I am not sensitive to praise." These assertions are so manifestly untrue that one can't help asking oneself how they could have become commonplace. It may be that so many people so often volunteer praise and criticism that is unfounded—knowingly or unknowingly—that laudatory and derogatory remarks in general have become suspect. We feel, and often rightly so, that flattery is used either just to be nice or to create goodwill through false pretenses in order to obtain a favor. Criticism may either reflect uncontrolled malice or provide an outlet for guilt feelings, an excuse for not being up to the standards whose value is therefore questioned. Naturally, no intelligent person should be influenced by this type of flattery or criticism, but we must not generalize our indifference to include honest and well-founded admiration or condemnation, both of which help us to find the way to a better and generally more acceptable conduct. Only the indolent vegetable type does not care about the impression he makes and the feelings he incites in others. By flaunting his indifference, he not only admits being worthless to society—a parasite on those who wish to make life pleasant—but he shows that he is so insensitive as to regard his attitude as something to be proud of.

Here, I must again return to one of my basic themes, the unjust criticism of conduct dictated by unassailable laws of Nature, first among which are all forms of egotism. Whatever the sages may say, as long as life persists on this planet, egotism must remain a fundamental guideline of conduct; were it to become obsolete, life itself would disappear.

A world in which each creature refuses to protect itself is unimaginable, but so is a world in which uncontrolled egotism with total disregard for the interests of others is the leading principle of behavior. To my mind, the only philosophy which necessarily transforms all aggressive egotistic impulses into altruism, without curtailing any of their self-protecting values, is altruistic egotism. It has amply proved its value throughout evolution from the simplest multicellular organism to man. In lower animals, whenever it developed, it was of considerable help but, being unpremeditated, could arise only through the power of its survival value. Wherever it developed—be it even by accident—it created new strengths which increased resistance.

Now my thesis is that man, with his most highly developed central nervous system, can consciously use his mind to direct his actions according to the laws of Nature; and once he fully understands the philosophy of egotistic altruism, he is no longer ashamed of being an egotist. He admits to being self-centered and acts primarily for his own good; he greedily collects a fortune to assure his personal freedom and capacity for survival under the most satisfying conditions, but he does so through amassing an army of friends. No one will make personal enemies if his egotism, his compulsive hoarding of valuables, manifests itself only by inciting love, goodwill, gratitude, respect, and all other positive feelings that render him useful and often indispensable to his neighbors.

Of course, it is easier to give than to take this kind of advice. If it were fully accepted by everyone, we would have paradise on earth; life would be governed only by human warmth and fellowship. There would be no wars, no crimes, no flights from the reality of unbearable life situations by drunkenness, narcotics, or even suicide. Who would want to escape from paradise?

I am painfully aware that we are very far from this state of general beatitude, and much as I have tried to present the means for reaching it in these pages, my efforts in themselves will certainly not suffice to make altruistic egotism a generally accepted common way of life. However, an ancient proverb says that even a journey of a thousand miles must start with a single step, and perhaps my attempt will stimulate others to propagate and develop these ideas. In any event, all that I have said here is not really new; it has been the basis of most religions and philosophies of conduct throughout the ages—expressed in one form or another by a variety of holy men, prophets, and sages who claimed to have arrived at various modifications of this natural code through inspiration. Often they even denied that these mysteries of supreme commands should be allowed dissection by critical intellect; they were to be accepted on faith. Perhaps, subconsciously, their exponents were afraid that the reasons they gave for altruism could not stand the acid test of step-by-step logical analysis.

All the ingredient ideas of my code have been known before, and many of them have been expressed more forcefully elsewhere. However, this lack of originality does not disturb me; it only reinforces my conviction that they are basic facts. The greatest truths which the structure of the human brain allows the mind to perceive and formulate have been expressed by wise men for thousands of years. All that the thinkers of any one period can do is to rediscover them under the thick layer of irrelevant trivialities in which they are constantly reburied by the dust of time, and then translate them into contemporary language.

Much more than this book will be needed to derive the whole benefit from the principle of altruistic egotism. Yet, I hope the thoughts expressed here will call attention to the fact that it is possible to arrive at a code which reconciles the timeless natural drives that, as long as they are in conflict, cause most of mankind's mental distress.

# 4

# To earn your neighbor's love

"Thou Shalt Love Thy Neighbor as Thyself"

Thus it is written in the Old Testament and re-emphasized by St. Matthew (Ch. 19, v. 19) and St. Mark (Ch. 12, v. 31); indeed, with certain variations, the same command can be found in the most diverse religions and philosophies. In fact, the golden rule, "Do unto others as you would have them do unto you," is only a modification of this command, but it still means you have to obey an unquestionable authority who orders you to love and be kind. Zoroaster taught it to the fire worshipers in Persia three thousand years ago. Confucius, Lao-Tse, and Buddha incorporated it

122

in their doctrines, and it reappears in Judaism and Christianity. It seems to have been formulated quite independently by numerous thinkers throughout the ages and throughout the world; hence, it undoubtedly has its roots deeply embedded in the human mind.

It is the earliest historic guideline designed to maintain equanimity and peace among men. If everyone loved his neighbor as himself, how could there be any war, crime, aggression, or even tension among people? In Biblical times, there was no better way of convincing the multitudes to be nice to each other than to issue this command. However, to follow it, one had to be unshakably convinced that it was the wish of some divine master whose authority and wisdom were unquestionable.

The various religions which encouraged us to accept this command differed in many ways; in some respects, they even held strictly opposite views. Yet, the existence and authority of one divine master was accepted on faith by the adherents of every group, although each vehemently denied the existence of all other gods. Fortunately, the devotees of any one god usually knew very little about the teachings of other religions; hence, such contradictions and uncertainties did not unduly disturb them. As long as faith was strong enough, I think the basic idea of keeping peace among men could not have been expressed any better. The effort to "love thy neighbor as thyself" probably has done more good, and more to make life pleasant, than any other guideline.

The only trouble is that strict adherence to such behavior is incompatible with the laws of biology. As I have said previously, whether we like it or not, egotism is an essential feature of all living beings, and, if we are honest with ourselves, we must admit that none of us actually loves all our fellow men as much as ourselves. When interests clash, I cannot expect others to take my interests as much to heart as their own.

Far be it from me to condemn the dictum "Thou shalt love thy neighbor as thyself," especially since I am convinced that it has long been most useful to humanity as a personal goal to strive for. But as the philosophical outlook and knowledge of man have developed since Biblical times, more and more of us have asked ourselves: How do we know who formulated this command, and is it really possible to follow it?

Frankly, I for one cannot abide by it. When I was younger I really tried hard, but I soon found that, try as I might, I could not love my neighbor as much as myself . . . even if success had not depended so much on the nature of my neighbor. With some of them—very few—I can come quite close to following the command, but I would be lying if I tried to convince myself that with more effort I might succeed in following it as a general law. When it comes to an obnoxious aggressive enemy who makes every effort to destroy me and all the things I believe in, and when I think of the lazy drunkard who lives as a parasite off the efforts of others, or of an incorrigible criminal and corrupter of youth, I feel it would be most unnatural for me to love him as much as myself or even as much as some of my truly lovable relatives or friends. Actually, I cannot succeed in loving even my most lovable neighbor as much as myself. In the extremely remote eventuality that I would have to decide whether my neighbor's or my life should be saved, I would choose my own. There are exceptions to this (a parent may not hesitate to die in order to save a child from a burning building), but—let us admit it—they are rare and cannot justify this type of behavior as a general guideline for conduct.

So why go on with this pretense? The self-deception leads only to feelings of inferiority; it gives us a bad conscience for not acting according to our avowed principles. And it is no satisfactory solution to say *mea culpa* and admit (even though with an undertone of righteous honesty) that you are an unworthy miserable sinner. Besides, I do not consider myself an unworthy miserable sinner. I think that, on the contrary, within the limits of my innate gifts, I have spared no effort to become a respected physician and scientist. I had to work hard for this all my life, and I continue to do so. I have tried to earn the satisfaction of being able to hold my head high in the conviction that I am doing my utmost to give meaning to my life through useful work. I refuse to lie about this. If I thought I were a despicable miserable sinner, I would get no satisfaction from merely confessing it; instead, I would immediately change my ways and try to deserve the respect and love of my neighbors.

I am convinced that without rejecting the principle "Love thy neighbor" we can adapt it to conform with biological laws discovered in our time and still be compatible with, yet independent of, any particular religion or political creed. As adapted, it neither presupposes nor excludes the existence of an infallible commander whose orders must be blindly followed. And, most important, it does not deny the essentially egotistic nature of living creatures. All that is needed is a simple rewording of the dictum.

## "Earn Thy Neighbors Love"

Thus expressed, we need not offer love on command to people who are truly unlovable; we need not love others as much as ourselves, which would be contrary to the laws of biology. Now success is up to us! Not all of us will be equally good at it, but, even so, the effort to follow the principle will give us a purpose for work; as we have seen, the human body is so constructed that, to maintain its physical and mental health, it must work for a purpose which can be accepted as worth the effort.

But in order to understand fully the dictum "Earn thy neighbor's love"—whether interpreted as a divine command reworded or as a sound biological law (and indeed the two interpretations are not mutually exclusive, for the laws of Nature are divine creations)—we must first come to grips with three questions:

1. What is love?
2. Who is your neighbor?
3. How can you earn love?

As mentioned earlier, I think that, according to the spirit of the Biblical command, the term "love" includes all positive feelings towards a person—certainly not only the almost instinctive love between man and woman or parents and children, but also the feeling of gratitude, friendship, admiration, compassion, and respect—in other words, goodwill. In any event, it is in this broad meaning that I am using the term here.

By "neighbor" I mean anyone close to me, including not only geographic but also genetic and —mainly—spiritual and intellectual proximity. In this general sense, the terms neighbor and brother are often used interchangeably, and I have tried to emphasize my view of this relationship in my book *From Dream to Discovery* by the question: "For who is my brother? The man of my blood, even if we have nothing else in common—or the man of my mind to whom I am bound only by the warmth of mutual understanding and common ideals?"

To make the motto "Earn thy neighbor's love" valuable, the goodwill of those who are physically or intellectually closest to us is most important, but the greater our contribution, the broader will be the neighborhood whose goodwill we can earn. An accomplishment like Einstein's theory of relativity won him the goodwill of nearly the entire human race.

But in order to earn your neighbor's love, you do not have to be an Einstein. For anybody, the best and simplest guide to accomplish this aim is to make himself as useful as possible. Of course, nobody is completely indispensable—but there are degrees. The sudden disappearance of some people would pass unnoticed, whereas the loss of others would be a serious blow to many. I think that the security and the feeling of fulfillment that we can earn, by becoming increasingly more necessary to our neighbors, are directly proportionate to the degree of our success. Although indispensability is never complete, working towards approximating it gives us a feeling of purpose, and represents the best way of earning love.

By helping them, you not only earn your neighbors' love, but also earn more neighbors. Isn't this why people adopt children? The main gratification of adopting children is that it furnishes us with the purpose of earning their love.

A charming true-life story illustrates how even very simple people can have the wisdom to realize that the love of your neighbors is much more likely to bring happiness than efficiency in your work. It was brought to my attention by Professor U. S. von Euler, who was awarded the Nobel Prize for his outstanding work on adrenalin and similar hormones which participate in stress reactions. In a letter commenting on a preliminary draft of this book, he wrote:

> On the train over the Andes, between Mendoza and Santiago, I sat talking to a Bolivian farmer, and asked him whether he utilized modern fertilizers to increase his harvests. "Oh, no," he said, "that would only create dissatisfaction in my neighbors. I prefer a modest harvest to be on good terms with them." You may say he earned the love of his neighbors by not trying to be too efficient.

I admire this farmer's wisdom because, in all honesty, I seriously doubt that I would have the strength to imitate him in my own field. If I knew a simple answer to something that puzzled a young graduate student, I often allowed him the satisfaction of proving that he could work it out himself, but when it came to my peers, I am afraid my desire to show off my superiority always got the better of me.

Finally, never forget that the only treasure that is yours forever is your ability to earn the love of your neighbors. Unpredictable social changes can suddenly deprive you of all the money, real estate, or political power that you were able to accumulate, but what you have learned is yours for life and is your safest investment. Work on that. Lost wars, social upheavals, and political changes have deprived—and continue to deprive—some of the mightiest of all their possessions overnight. History has shown us again and again that thousands of powerful aristocrats, eminent members of religious, political, or racial groups have suddenly become destitute after an unpredictable event made their privileges worthless. Among them, only those escaped this fate who had always invested in themselves, in their own ability to earn their neighbor's love.

I have always advised my children and students not to worry so much about saving money or about climbing up to the next rung on the ladder of their career, an attitude which seems to be an obsession with highly motivated people, concerned about economic security. It is much more important to work at perfecting yourself and thereby ensure your usefulness no matter what fate does to you. A great economist, artist, or scientist, or a first-rate machinist or plumber rarely has difficulty finding a job if some political or religious persecution drives him out of his country penniless. Remember that no matter what your degree or title, your highest rank is the reputation of your name. You are as valuable and secure as past accomplishments and present capabilities have helped to make you; in other words, you are worth as much as your ability to earn your neighbor's love.

# 5

# Résumé

This last chapter will attempt (1) to state concisely what we can expect from a code primarily designed to earn goodwill and (2) to re-evaluate the extent to which it is based on scientific facts rather than on mere intuitive or traditional trust in certain precepts.

## OBJECTIVES OF OUR GUIDELINES

*To supply us with purpose.* Our code offers a worthwhile aim whose utility to ourselves and to others is evident. To earn goodwill helps all and hurts nobody. It provides great security; having shown our usefulness and gained the goodwill, gratitude, and confidence of our potential enemies, why would they want to attack us?

*To provide a natural code of ethics.* We need guidelines of behavior which are compatible with the ruthless laws of biology and yet remain morally acceptable to ourselves and to other humane human beings. Only the nobility of our final aim, to gain personal satisfaction by helping others, can justify such unsavory but inescapable biological drives as egotism and the urge to greedily hoard possessions. Last but not least, the impossibility of achieving absolute perfection through this code—the acquisition of everybody's undivided love—provides unlimited scope for constant improvement, the only permanent guideline for conduct.

## THE BIOLOGICAL ROOTS OF OUR CODE

*Nonspecificity vs. specificity.* My work on stress, which was discussed in Chapter 1, clearly indicates the need to distinguish between nonspecific and specific features, since objective experiments have shown that every stimulus or event (drugs, traumatic injury, social problems) produces nonspecific stress, in addition to the specific effects characteristic of each one of them. Therefore, we must get used to regarding all problems we face as combinations of several factors. Among these, it is often difficult, without conscious search, to identify the determining one that should be selected or avoided.

Whether an athletic effort merely strengthens

our muscles or produces a heart attack depends upon a host of factors, some inherited, some environmental. Our experimental studies on "pluricausal diseases" have taught us that many maladies have no specific single cause but are the result of a constellation of factors, among which mere nonspecific stress often plays a decisive role. Similarly, many common diseases—peptic ulcers, high blood pressure, nervous breakdowns—may not be primarily due to such apparent causes as diet, genetics, or occupational hazards. They may merely be the nonspecific stress effects of attempting to endure more than we can. Here, instead of complicated drug therapies or surgical operations, we can often help ourselves better by identifying the decisive cause, which may be a member of our family, our boss, or merely our own overemphasis on the importance of being right every time.

*Altruistic egotism.* Egotism was the basis of evolution throughout the ages. The originally simplest forms of life, consisting of individual and totally independent cells, were subject to the relentless law of natural selection; those cells that could not protect themselves soon ceased to exist. It also became apparent, however, that such pure egocentricity created dangerous antagonisms, the advantages of one individual often being acquired to the detriment of others. Therefore, a certain degree of altruism had to be introduced for egotistic reasons. Unicellular organisms began to aggregate and form stronger, more complex multicellular beings; in these, certain cells had to give up part of their independence to specialize in nutrition, defense, or locomotion, but thereby the security and survival value of each individual were raised.

I have emphasized—perhaps irritatingly often—that egotism is an inherent and unavoidable characteristic of life. Yet pure egotism necessarily leads to conflict and insecurity within the community. Sometimes, brutal sacrifice is indispensable to protect living Nature as a whole. In battle, a general must occasionally reach the painful decision of sacrificing a platoon, or even a regiment, to save an army. But the most efficient and pleasant way of combining the advantages of the few with those of the many is the principle of altruistic egotism.

Single cells combined into multicellular organisms and these into larger groups on the basis of this principle, although they were not aware of it. Similarly, individual people have formed the co-operative "mutual insurance" groups of the family, tribes, and nations within which altruistic egotism is the key to success. It is the only way to preserve teamwork, whose value is ever increasing in modern society.

*The triphasic nature of adaptability.* We have shown that animals exposed to continuous stress for long periods necessarily go through the three phases of the G.A.S.: the initial alarm reaction, followed by resistance and, eventually, exhaustion. Evidently adaptability, or adaptation energy, is a finite amount of vitality given to us at birth. It is comparable to inherited capital from which we can withdraw throughout life, but to which we cannot add. In terms of the adaptation energy consumed by the stress of life, the secret of success is not to avoid stress and thereby endure an uneventful, boring life, for then our wealth would do us no good, but to learn to use our capital wisely, to get maximal satisfaction at the lowest price. Often, the satisfaction of any experience must be bought at the price of sacrificing another. It pays to learn how not to squander this valuable asset on futilities.

*Activity is a biological necessity.* We have seen that unused muscles, brains, and other organs lose efficiency. To keep fit, we must exercise both our bodies and our minds. Besides, inactivity deprives us of every outlet for our innate urge to create, to build; this causes tensions and the insecurity that stems from aimlessness. Whether we call our activity exhausting work or relaxing play depends largely upon our own attitude towards it. We should at least get on friendly terms with our job; ideally, we should try to find "play professions" that are as pleasant, useful, and constructive as possible. These should give us the best outlets—safety valves—for self-realization, and for preventing irrational, violent outbreaks or flight into the dream life of drugs such as occur in people whose high motivation is frustrated by the lack of an acceptable aim. In seeking a worthwhile goal, remember my little jingle: "*Fight for your highest attainable aim / but never put up resistance in vain.*" In other words, it won't hurt you to work hard for something you want, but make sure that it is really you who wants it—not merely your society, parents, teachers, neighbors—and that you can be a winner.

Remember also that, in most instances, diversion from one activity to another is more relaxing than complete rest. Few things are as frustrating as complete inactivity, the absence of any stimulus, any challenge, to which you could react.

As a physician, I have seen innumerable instances of this in patients who suffered from some incapacitating, painful, and incurable disease. Those who sought relief in complete rest suffered most because they could not avoid thinking constantly about their hopeless future, whereas those who managed to go on being active as long as possible gained strength from solving the many little tasks of daily life which took their minds off more sinister considerations. Few things would give more help to the hopeless than to teach them to exploit the healing stress of diversion.

*Choose carefully between syntoxic and catatoxic behavior in daily life.* The most impressive biochemical observations in experiments on syntoxic and catatoxic hormones revealed the importance of the choice between submission and attack; in chemical language, these hormones carry the message to put up with the aggressor or to fight it. This choice is of vital importance on all levels of biological organization, from single cells all the way to man, families of men, and even nations. You cannot trust emotion always to choose correctly. It helps a great deal to understand the fundamental advantages and disadvantages of both attitudes by studying the biological basis of self-preservation as reflected in the syntoxic and catatoxic chemical mechanisms. When applied to everyday problems, this understanding should lead to choices most likely to provide us with the pleasant stress of fulfillment and victory, thereby avoiding the self-destructive distress of failure, frustration, hatred, and the passion for revenge.

*The general acceptability of our code.* I have tried to support my guidelines mainly by modern biological experiments, but they are also in harmony with time-honored principles of various religions and philosophies. With very few exceptions, only those teachings that are deeply rooted in human nature survive indefinitely. The trust in the all-powerful, eternal creative force of some divinity goes back to the beginnings of recorded history, but its many forms are all alike in one respect: they try to provide us with guidelines for conduct that lead to an ultimate goal.

Some religions and philosophies have become obsolete; many others continue to exert a powerful influence upon man's behavior. However, the basic objective is still to achieve internal peace within man and external peace among men, as well as between man and Nature.

Whatever trends toward change have occurred are mainly limited to the justification of conduct. Since people got sick from eating pork long before it was realized that pigs often suffer from a disease called trichinosis, the best way to make people avoid pork was to call swine dirty animals, unpleasing to God. Before we knew that, especially in hot climates, almost anything we touched was likely to be infected with dangerous bacteria, the best way to ward off epidemics was to recommend careful ritual ablutions before every meal. But irrespective of the reasons given, such laws persisted because they proved to be useful.

"Love thy neighbor as thyself," one of the oldest guidelines for purpose and conduct, was propounded to please God and offer security to man. Since our philosophy is based on natural laws, it is perhaps not surprising that, for centuries, throughout the world, so many of its elements have turned up again and again—in the most diverse religions and political doctrines—though usually supported by mysticism rather than by science. The people in whose cultures one or the other of these elements appeared were quite unrelated and often did not even know of each other's existence. Their creeds had only one thing in common: they were the creations of the human brain and reflected the natural evolution of its functional mechanism.

This is perhaps why our updated guideline, "Earn thy neighbor's love," cannot conflict with any religion or philosophy; in fact, ardent believers in one of these can use our code to complement their own. In it, they will find scientific support not only for one of the most deep-rooted and generally accepted religious precepts of the brotherhood of man but also for that of atheistic communism, with its avowed goal: "From each according to his capacities, to each according to his needs," a slogan which otherwise might only encourage laziness. The laws of Nature, which we used to construct our doctrine, apply to everybody, irrespective of his formalized and labeled creed.

Viewed from the pinnacle of the eternal general laws governing Nature, we are all surprisingly alike. Nature is the fountainhead of all our problems and solutions; the closer we keep to her the better we realize that, despite the apparently enormous divergencies in interpretation and explanation, her laws have always prevailed and can never become obsolete. The realization of this truth is most likely to convince us that, in a sense, not only all men but all living beings are brothers. To avoid the stress of conflict, frustration, and hate, to achieve peace and happiness, we should devote more attention to a better understanding of the natural basis of motivation and behavior. No one will be disappointed if, in daily life, he learns to follow the guiding light of "Earn thy neighbor's love."

*Prescription for enjoying a full life.* We have seen that the stress of frustration is particularly harmful. Man, with his highly developed central nervous system, is especially vulnerable to psychic insults, and there are various little tricks to minimize these. Here are a few that I have found useful:

Even if you systematically want to hoard love, don't waste your time trying to befriend a mad dog.

Admit that there is no perfection, but in each category of achievement something is tops; be satisfied to strive for that.

Do not underestimate the delight of real simplicity in your life style. Avoidance of all affectations and unnecessary complications earns as much goodwill and love as pompous artificiality earns dislike.

Whatever situation you meet in life, consider first whether it is really worth fighting for. Do not forget what Nature has taught us about the importance of carefully adjusting syntoxic and catatoxic attitudes to any problems of a cell, a man, or even a society.

Try to keep your mind constantly on the pleasant aspects of life and on actions which can improve your situation. Try to forget everything that is irrevocably ugly or painful. This is perhaps the most efficient way of minimizing stress by what I have called voluntary mental diversion. As a wise German proverb says, "Imitate the sundial's ways; / Count only the pleasant days."

Nothing paralyzes your efficiency more than frustration; nothing helps it more than success. Even after the greatest defeats the depressing thought of being a failure is best combatted by taking stock of all your past achievements which no one can deny you. Such conscious stock-taking is most effective in re-establishing the self-confidence necessary for future success. There is something even in the most modest career that we are proud to recall—you would be surprised to see how much this can help when everything seems hopeless.

When faced with a task which is very painful yet indispensable to achieve your aim, don't procrastinate; cut right into an abscess to eliminate the pain, instead of prolonging it by gently rubbing the surface.

Realize that men are not created equal, though they should, of course, have a birthright to equal opportunities. After birth, in a free society, their performance should determine their progress. There will always be leaders and followers, but the leaders are worth keeping only as long as they can serve the followers by acquiring their love, respect, and gratitude.

Finally, do not forget that there is no ready-made success formula which would suit everybody. We are all different and so are our problems. The only thing we have in common is our subordination to those fundamental biological laws which govern all living beings, including man. Hence, I think a natural code of behavior based on non-specific mechanisms of adaptation comes closest to what can be offered as a general guideline for conduct.

I myself have tried to follow the philosophy of earning my neighbor's love as best I could, and it has made my life a happy one. Let me frankly admit that, in looking back, I realize that I have not always succeeded to perfection, but my failures were due to my own shortcomings, not to those of the philosophy itself. The inventor of the best racing car is not necessarily its best driver.

In closing, let me express the wish that many of you who read these pages will be better at applying my principles than I am, for I should like your success to augment my capital of love, gratitude, and goodwill, which I have so shamelessly admitted wanting to hoard.

*And one might therefore say of me that in this book I have only made up a bunch of other people's flowers, and that of my own I have only provided the string that ties them together.*

*—Montaigne*

# Glossary

*acetylcholine.* A substance transmitting certain nervous impulses.

*ACTH.* Abbreviation for adrenocorticotrophic hormone.

*adaptation energy.* The energy necessary to acquire and maintain adaptation, apart from caloric requirements.

*adaptive hormones.* Hormones produced for adaptation.

*adrenalin.* One of the hormones secreted by the adrenal medulla. A derivative of it (noradrenalin) transmits certain nervous impulses.

*adrenals.* Two endocrine glands situated just above the kidneys. They consist of a whitish outer cortex, or bark (which produces corticoids), and a dark brown medulla, or marrow (which makes adrenalin).

*adrenocorticotrophic hormone (ACTH)*. A pituitary hormone which stimulates the growth and function of the adrenal cortex.

*alarm reaction*. The first stage of the general adaptation syndrome. In the G.A.S., it affects the body as a whole.

*antibiotics*. Antibacterial substances, most of which are prepared from molds or fungi (e.g., penicillin, streptomycin).

*anti-inflammatory corticoids*. Adrenocortical hormones which inhibit inflammation, for example, cortisone or cortisol. They have a marked effect upon glucose metabolism and are therefore also known as glucocorticoids.

*atrophy*. Shrinkage of an organ. See also *involution*

*catatoxic (cata=against)*. Substances which attack damaging agents, e.g., by inducing enzymes which destroy toxic compounds.

*cell*. A relatively autonomous, circumscribed, small mass of living material, visible under the microscope. The tissues of all living beings consist mainly of cells.

*conditioning factors*. Substances or circumstances which influence the response to an agent, for instance, a hormone.

*connective tissue*. A tissue consisting of cells and

fine fibers; it is a kind of living cement which connects and reinforces all other tissues. Inflammation develops mainly in connective tissue.

*corticoids*. Hormones of the adrenal cortex. It is customary to subdivide them into anti-inflammatory glucocorticoids and pro-inflammatory mineralocorticoids.

*direct pathogen*. An agent which causes disease by its own inherent actions, not merely by stimulating abnormal responses in living beings, e.g., a strong acid, physical injury, or extreme temperatures, which traumatize, burn, or freeze tissues.

*diseases of adaptation*. Maladies which are principally due to imperfections of the G.A.S., for instance, to an excessive or insufficient amount, or to an improper mixture, of adaptive hormones.

*distress*. Harmful, unpleasant stress.

*endocrines*. Ductless glands which secrete their products (hormones) directly into the blood.

*enzyme*. A naturally occurring substance, formed by living cells, which accelerates certain chemical reactions.

*extract*. A preparation obtained by mixing tissue (e.g., liver, ovary, muscle, or combination of chemicals) with solvents (e.g., water, alcohol) and then recovering the soluble material.

*feedback*. The return of some of the output of a system as input.

*G.A.S.* General adaptation syndrome.

*general adaptation syndrome*. The manifestations of stress in the whole body, as they develop in time. The general adaptation syndrome evolves in three distinct stages: alarm reaction, stage of resistance, stage of exhaustion.

*genes*. Minute intracellular particles which act as code letters of a chemical alphabet. Through them, hereditary information can be transmitted to successive generations.

*heterostasis (heteros*=other; *stasis*=position). The establishment of a new steady state by treatments which stimulate normally dormant capacities of homeostasis, raising them to maintain a heightened level of resistance.

*histology*. The study of the minute microscopic structure of tissues.

*homeostasis (homoios*=similar and *stasis*=position). The body's tendency to maintain a steady state despite external changes; physiological "staying power."

*hormones*. Chemical substances released into the blood by the endocrine glands to stimulate and coordinate distant organs. Bodily growth, metabolism, resistance to stress, inflammation, and sexual functions are largely regulated by hormones.

*hypophysis*. See *pituitary*

*hypothalamus*. A brain region at the base of the skull, from which messages go to the hypophysis, e.g., to secrete ACTH during stress.

*indirect pathogen*. An essentially innocuous agent which causes damage by evoking inappropriate defense reactions; then only the latter are experienced as disease (e.g., allergic inflammation, excessive mental irritation and tension).

*inflammation*. The typical reaction of tissue (particularly of connective tissue) to injury. Its main purpose is to seal off injurious agents.

*involution*. Natural shrinkage or decline of an organ. See also *atrophy*

*lesion*. A pathological change in bodily structure.

*lymphatic tissues*. Tissues containing mainly lymph cells (e.g., in the thymus, in lymph nodes).

*lymph nodes*. Nodular organs, consisting of lymphatic tissue, in the groin, under the armpits, along the neck, and in various parts of the body.

*milieu intérieur*. The internal environment of the body; the soil in which all biological reactions develop.

*nonspecific*. A nonspecifically formed change is one which affects all or most parts of a system without selectivity. It is the opposite of a specifically formed change, which affects only one or, at most, a few units within a system. A nonspecifically caused change is one which can be produced by many or all agents.

*nonspecific therapy.* Treatment which is beneficial in various kinds of maladies and not directed against any one pathogen.

*noradrenalin.* One of the hormones secreted by the adrenal medulla.

*ovaries.* The female sex glands.

*pathogen.* An agent which causes disease. See also *direct pathogen; indirect pathogen*

*pathology.* The study of disease.

PCN. Pregnenolone-16$a$-carbonitrile, a powerful catatoxic hormone derivative.

*pituitary.* A little endocrine gland embedded in the bones of the skull just below the brain; also known as *hypophysis.*

*reaction.* In biology, the response of the body, or of one of its parts, to stimulation.

*shock therapy.* Treatment with shocks elicited by drugs or electricity.

*specific.* A specifically formed change is one which affects only a single unit or, at most, a few units within a system, with great selectivity. A specifically caused change is one which can be produced only by a single agent or, at most, by a few agents. The term *specific* has no meaning unless we indicate whether it refers to the change itself or to its causation.

*stage of exhaustion.* The final stage of the general adaptation syndrome.

*stage of resistance.* The second stage of the general adaptation syndrome.

*stimulus.* In biology, anything that elicits a reaction in the body or in one of its parts.

*stress.* In biology, the nonspecific response of the body to any demand made upon it. For general orientation, it suffices to keep in mind that by stress the physician means the common results of exposure to any stimulus. For example, the bodily changes produced whether a person is exposed to nervous tension, physical injury, infection, cold, heat, X rays, or anything else are what we call stress. In other words, stress is what remains when we disregard specific changes. In my earlier writings, I had defined stress, somewhat more simply but less precisely, as the "sum of all nonspecific changes caused by function or damage," or "the rate of wear and tear in the body. See also *distress*

*stressor.* That which produces stress.

*symbiosis (sym=*together; *boisis=*living). The mutually advantageous association of two or more individuals of different species; e.g., the growth of certain bacteria in the cow's rumen, which permit the grass consumed to be better digested by the cow, at the same time providing nourishment and shelter for the microbes.

*syndrome*. A group of symptoms and signs which appear together.

*synergy*. Cooperative action.

*syntoxic* (*syn*=together). Syntoxic substances act as tissue tranquilizers, creating a state of passive tolerance which permits peaceful coexistence with aggressors. Thereby, they can eliminate those disease manifestations which are principally due to excessive responses of our body, e.g., inflammation.

*therapy*. Treatment.

*thymicolymphatic apparatus*. A system consisting of the thymus and lymph nodes.

*thymus*. A large lymphatic organ in the chest.

*tissue*. In biology, a collection of cells and the intercellular material surrounding them.

*triad*. A syndrome consisting of three manifestations.

*triphasic*. Having, or developing in, three stages, as the G.A.S.

*ulcer*. Inflammation and erosion on a surface.

# Bibliography

PRINCIPAL PUBLICATIONS UPON WHICH THIS ESSAY
    IS BASED

Bernard, C. *Introduction à l'étude de la médecine
    expérimentale*. Paris: Editions Flammarion,
    1945.
Cannon, W. B. *The Wisdom of the Body*. New
    York: W. W. Norton & Co., 1932.
Selye, H. *Stress*. Montreal: Acta, Inc., 1950.
——. *The Stress of Life*. New York, Toronto, Lon-
    don: McGraw-Hill Book Co., Inc., 1956.
——. *The Chemical Prevention of Cardiac Necro-
    sis*. New York: Ronald Press Co., 1958.
——. *The Pluricausal Cardiopathies*. Springfield,
    Ill.: Charles C. Thomas, Publisher, 1961.

——. *Calciphylaxis*. Chicago: University of Chicago Press, 1962.

——. *From Dream to Discovery: On Being a Scientist*. New York, Toronto, London: McGraw-Hill Book Co., Inc., 1964.

——. *In Vivo: The Case for Supramolecular Biology*. New York: Liveright Publishing Corporation, 1967.

——. *Experimental Cardiovascular Diseases*. 2 vols. New York, Heidelberg, Berlin: Springer-Verlag, 1970.

——. "Stress and Aging." *J. Amer. Geriat. Soc.* 18 (1970): 669–680.

——. *Hormones and Resistance*. 2 vols. New York, Heidelberg, Berlin: Springer-Verlag, 1971.

——. "Homeostasis and Heterostasis." *Perspect. Biol. Med.* 16 (1973): 441–445.

——, and coworkers. *Annual Reports on Stress*. Montreal: Acta, Inc., 1951–1956.

## ADDITIONAL ANNOTATED REFERENCES

To keep this volume as readable as possible, only the highlights of what is known about stress have been presented in simple terms. For those interested in more information on specific aspects (described in lay or technical language), I have chosen and annotated the following key references (from among approximately 80,000 titles of our documentation on stress in the library of the Institute of Experimental Medicine and Surgery); most of them are books or reviews which quote much additional literature on special topics. Inclusion of a title does not imply approval. On the contrary, many of the references were selected purposely to represent different and sometimes conflicting points of view. Among these titles, students and teachers will easily find detailed texts on stress in relation to such varied subjects as biochemistry, psychosomatics, business, aerospace medicine, surgery, geriatrics, noise pollution, genetic predisposition, and interpersonal relations.

Abram, H. S., ed. *Psychological Aspects of Stress.* Springfield, Ill.: Charles C. Thomas, Publisher, 1970. Proceedings of a symposium sponsored by the University of Virginia School of Medicine and Medical Education for National Defense (MEND). Seven specialists in different aspects of stress discuss psychological and physiological reactions to extremely stressful situations such as disasters, life-threatening illness, combat, life in concentration camps, and outer space.

Alexander, F. *Psychosomatic Medicine.* New York: W. W. Norton & Co., Inc., 1950. Simple textbook on psychosomatic medicine in relation to psychoanalysis and the G.A.S. (260 refs.).

Appley, M. H., and Trumbull, R., eds. *Psychological Stress: Issues in Research.* New York: Appleton-Century-Crofts, 1967. Conference on psychological stress, York University, Toronto, Canada, with the participation of numerous specialists who gave papers on the technical aspects of the G.A.S. in relation to psychosomatic medicine.

Archer, J. E., and Blackman, D. E. "Prenatal Psychological Stress and Offspring Behavior in Rats and Mice." *Develop. Psychobiol.* 4 (1971): 193–248. Extensive review of the literature and many interesting personal observations on the effect upon the offspring of stress applied to the mother. The results permit few conclusions except that some change in activity-reactivity may be thus induced (numerous refs.).

Association for Research in Nervous and Mental Disease. *Life Stress and Bodily Disease; Proceedings of the Association, Dec. 2 and 3, 1949.* Edited by H. G. Wolff, S. G. Wolf, Jr., and C. C. Hare. Baltimore: The Williams & Wilkins Co., 1950. The proceedings include papers on: mechanisms involved in reactions to stress; the problem of specificity; life stress; headaches; disorders of growth, development, and metabolism; diseases of the eye, respiratory passages, gastrointestinal tract, locomotor apparatus, cardiovascular system, skin, and genital organs.

Bajusz, E., ed. *Physiology and Pathology of Adaptation Mechanisms*. Oxford, London, Edinburgh: Pergamon Press, 1969. Technical monograph with independent articles by numerous specialists in adaptation. One large section deals with "The Pituitary Adrenocortical System, Its Regulation and Adaptive Functions," and another with "Regulation of 'Adaptive Hormones,' Other than ACTH." Additional presentations are concerned with neuroendocrine regulatory adaptation mechanisms and adaptation to changes in environmental temperature.

Baron, R. A. *The Tyranny of Noise*. New York, Evanston, Ill., San Francisco, London: Harper & Row, Publishers, 1971. Very readable summary on the price you pay for the stressor effect of various types of noise characteristic of our civilization. Special attention is given to the noise of urban life, the abusive use of technology, and aviation. Statistics on noise in terms of health and dollars. Technical means to avoid or minimize noise.

Bartley, S. H., and Chute, E. *Fatigue and Impairment in Man*. Foreword by A. C. Ivy.

New York, London: McGraw-Hill Book Co., Inc., 1947. Monograph on various types of specific organ system impairments and general fatigue. A wealth of empirical information without any reference to the stress concept.

Basowitz, H.; Persky, H.; Horchin, S. J.; and Grinker, R. R. *Anxiety and Stress.* New York, Toronto, London: McGraw-Hill Book Co., Inc., 1954. Well-documented monograph on anxiety, especially in relation to stress and the G.A.S.

Bourne, P. G., ed. *The Psychology and Physiology of Stress.* New York: Academic Press, Inc., 1969. Stress with special reference to observations made during the Vietnam war. Most of the contributors were active army physicians who dealt with psychiatric problems of combat stress, heat stress in army pilots, stress and fatigue-monitoring of naval aviators. Interesting data on corticoid and androgen excretion as influenced by combat situations.

Bovard, E. W. "The Effects of Social Stimuli on the Response to Stress." *Physiol. Rev.* 66 (1959): 267–277. Brief semipopular summary of the effect of social stimuli on the response to stress, with emphasis upon the interactions between various parts of the nervous system and the secretion of stress hormones during the G.A.S.

Buckley, J. P. "Physiological Effects of Environmental Stimuli." *J. Pharm. Sci.* 61 (1972): 1175–1188. Highly constructive and critical evaluation of the present status of the stress concept, based on technical literature (158 refs.).

Bugard, P. *La Fatigue*. Paris: Masson & Cie. Editeurs, 1960. Somewhat technical discussion on the somatic and psychic manifestations of fatigue, with reference to the G.A.S. In French.

Calloway, D. H., ed. *Human Ecology in Space Flight II*. New York: New York Academy of Sciences, 1966. Symposium on the medical aspects of space flight with special emphasis on the stressor effect of high G forces, motion sickness, variations in temperature, toxic gases, ionizing rays, life in a magnetic field, and emotional factors; and particularly on the combined stressor action of several among these factors.

Cannon, W. B. *Bodily Changes in Pain, Hunger, Fear and Rage*. Boston: Charles T. Branford Co., 1953. Excellent summary of the author's classic observations on the somatic manifestations of acute emotions, particularly with regard to the effect of fear, rage, hunger, and thirst upon the sympathetic nervous system and adrenaline secretion.

Cohen, B. M., and Cooper, M. Z. *A Follow-up Study of World War II Prisoners of War.* Washington, D.C.: Veterans Administration Medical Monograph, 1954. Statistical analysis by the U.S. Army of white male survivors of imprisonment by the Japanese and Germans during World War II, with special emphasis on after-effects (morbidity, mortality) following liberation or escape. Although extensive data suggest lasting unfavorable after-effects, evaluation of the role of stress as such or of more specific factors (malnutrition, infection, trauma) is difficult.

Corson, S. A. "Neuroendocrine and Behavorial Response Patterns to Psychologic Stress and the Problem of the Target Tissue in Cerebrovisceral Pathology." *Ann. N.Y. Acad. Sci.* 125 (1966): 890–918. Review of the technical literature on the conditioning factors determining the particular target tissue which will respond to physiological or psychological stresssors.

Curtis, H. J. *Biological Mechanism of Aging.* Springfield, Ill.: Charles C. Thomas, Publisher, 1966. Monograph on the biochemical basis of aging, with a special section on the stress theory.

Dill, D. B., and others, eds. *Adaptation to the Environment.* Handbook of Physiology, edited by John Field, section 4. Washington, D.C.: American Physiological Society, 1964. Encyclopedic treatise on adaptation to the most diverse environmental changes. Numerous sections deal with the role of the G.A.S.

Dunbar, F. *Emotions and Bodily Changes.* New York: Columbia University Press, 1947. Survey of the literature between 1910 and 1945 on psychosomatic interrelations (2,400 refs.).

Dunn, W. L., Jr., ed. *Smoking Behavior: Motives and Incentives.* Introduction by Hans Selye. New York: John Wiley & Sons, 1973. An international symposium on why people smoke, with special reference to the relaxation derived from this habit at times of mental tension.

Eitinger, L. *Concentration Camp Survivors in Norway and Israel.* 2d ed. The Hague: Martinus Nijhoff, 1964. A most instructive analysis of the subsequent fate of Nazi concentration camp inmates who after liberation continued their life either in Norway or in Israel; "to examine whether the severe psychic and physical stress situations to which human beings were exposed in the concentration camps of World War II have had lasting psychological results, to discover the nature of these conditions and the symptomatology they present, and finally to investigate which detailed factors of the above-mentioned stress situations can be considered decisive for the morbid conditions which were revealed."

——, and Strøm, A. *Mortality and Morbidity After Excessive Stress: A Follow-up Investigation of Norwegian Concentration Camp Survivors.* New York: Humanities Press, Inc., 1973. Further evaluation of the population described in the previously cited volume led to the conclusion that "the most natural explanation of the ex-prisoners' high mortality and morbidity is that the excessive stress they experienced during imprisonment lowered their resistance to infection and lessened their ability to adjust to environmental changes. . . . Other forms of stress may have similar effects on the organism and may contribute to the increase of 'stress diseases' in the modern world."

Engle, E. T., and Pincus, G., eds. *Hormones and the Aging Process.* New York: Academic Press, Inc., 1956. Proceedings of a conference. Many experts discussed the literature on hormones and aging in fairly technical language, well documented by references. One section, by D. J. Ingle, is specifically devoted to the role of stress in aging and the hormones produced during the G.A.S.

von Euler, U.S.; Gemzell, C. A.; Levi, L.; and Ström, G. "Cortical and Medullary Adrenal

Activity in Emotional Stress." *Acta Endo-crinol.* 30 (1959): 567–573. Brief technical note on cortical and medullary adrenal activity in emotional stress, based on new techniques of corticoid and adrenalinlike hormone determinations.

Farber, S. M.; Mustacchi, P.; and Wilson, R. H. L., eds. *Man Under Stress.* Berkeley, Los Angeles: University of California Press, 1964. Proceedings of a symposium organized by the University of California. A group of physicians, surgeons, and basic research men (among them Brock Chisholm, René Dubos, Seymour Farber, Stanley Sarnoff, Hans Selye, Paul Dudley White) discussed the various aspects of stress, particularly in relation to the philosophy of life, social environment, cardiovascular disease, space medicine, etc. Most of the speakers refrained from highly technical discussions, but key references to scientific papers are given.

Friedrich, R. *Tomorrow's Medicine: New Theories and Fields of Investigation* [Medizin von Morgen. Neue Theorien und Forschungsergebnisse]. Munich: Süddeutscher Verlag, 1955. A major portion of the volume is devoted to a description of stress and the G.A.S. in generally understandable terms. Special attention is given to the historical development of the stress concept. In German.

———, ed. Frontiers of Medicine. New York: Liveright Publishing Corporation, 1961. Popularization of various new concepts in medicine (antibiotics, artificial hibernation, sleep therapy, etc.), with one section entitled "A New System: Selye's Theories of Stress and Adaptation."

Funkenstein, D. H; King, S. H.; and Drolette, M. E. *Mastery of Stress*. Cambridge: Harvard University Press, 1957. Observations on stress-producing situations and their prevention in man and experimental animals. Main emphasis is laid upon psychological factors, but the somatic aspects of the G.A.S. are also considered.

Galdston, I. *Beyond the Germ Theory*. New York, Minneapolis: Health Education Council, 1954. Very readable book with major emphasis upon the disease-producing effects of "deprivation stress" in relation to the G.A.S. Special sections on deprivation of food and emotional stimuli.

Gauer, O. H., and Zuidema, G. D., eds. *Gravitational Stress in Aerospace Medicine*. Foreword by J. P. Stapp, Colonel, USAF (MC). Boston: Little, Brown & Co., 1961. Symposium sponsored by the Aerospace Medical Laboratory, Wright-Patterson Air Force Base, Ohio. Fourteen experts, mostly members of the USAF, discussed the psychic and somatic results of exposure to stress in aircraft and spaceships, with primary emphasis upon acceleration, deceleration, and weightlessness.

Giertsen, J. C. "Sudden Death from Natural Causes." *Arb. Univ. Bergen Med. Ser.*, no. 1 (1962), 1–52. Forensic implications of stress in death attributed to "natural causes."

Glass, D. C., and Singer, J. E. *Urban Stress: Experiments on Noise and Social Stressors.* New York, London: Academic Press, Inc., 1972. Monograph (about 120 refs.) on the stressor effect of noise, mainly as a function of predictability and subject control. Despite the title, little is said about other stressors in urban life, but the book—which earned its authors the 1971 Socio-Psychological Prize of the American Association for the Advancement of Science—undoubtedly contains many valuable data on human response to psychosocial stressors.

Grinker, R. R., and Spiegel, J. P. *Men Under Stress.* Philadelphia: The Blakiston Co., 1945. Extensive monograph on the stressor effects of combat upon U.S. troops during World War II. Special sections deal with genetic predisposing factors, the environment of combat, combat morale, reactions after combat, and applications to civilian psychiatry.

Gross, N. E. *Living With Stress*. Foreword by Hans Selye. New York, Toronto, London: McGraw-Hill Book Co., Inc., 1958. Summary, in lay language, of the stress concept and its application to daily life.

Halliday, J. L. *Psychosocial Medicine*. New York: W. W. Norton & Co., Inc., 1947. Popular volume on psychosocial medicine, with only occasional references to stress.

Hambling, J., ed. *The Nature of Stress Disorder*. Springfield, Ill.: Charles C. Thomas, 1959. Proceedings of the Conference of the Society for Psychosomatic Research at the Royal College of Physicians, London. Several experts discussed the G.A.S. on the basis of animal experiments and observations in man. Special sections deal with stress in aviation, skin disorders, gastrointestinal disease, industry, the family setting, and genetic predisposition.

Hill, R. "Generic Features of Families Under Stress." Social Stresses on the Family, I. *Social Casework* 39 (1958): 139–150. Interdisciplinary conference on the behavior of families under stress, jointly sponsored by the Family Service Association of America and the Elizabeth McCormick Memorial Fund. Analysis of the respective roles of stressor agents, hereditary predisposition, and interpersonal relationships which may affect adjustment to crises.

Special emphasis is placed upon advice to social agencies regarding policies and practice.

Howard, A., and Scott, R. A. "A Proposed Framework for the Analysis of Stress in the Human Organism." *Behav. Sci.* 10 (1965): 141–160. An encompassing theoretical scheme which "proposes to reduce the conceptual barriers between various biochemical, physical, psychological, and sociocultural models of stress." (Numerous references to the technical literature.)

Janis, I. L. *Psychological Stress.* New York: John Wiley & Sons, Inc., 1958. Psychoanalytical and behavioral studies of surgical patients, with reports of interviews before and after operations and an evaluation of the practical lessons to be drawn from them.

Jensen, J. *Modern Concepts in Medicine.* St. Louis: The C. V. Mosby Co., 1953. Voluminous treatise which attempts to reinterpret virtually the whole of physiology, biochemistry, and medicine using the G.A.S. as a unifying concept. Very painstaking compilation of data interpreted in a somewhat daringly speculative manner.

Kennedy, J. A. *Relax and Live.* Englewood Cliffs, N. J.: Prentice-Hall, Inc., 1953. Advice on how to relax and avoid disease, given in lay language. One section is devoted to the relationship between aging and the G.A.S.

Kerner, F. *Stress and Your Heart.* Introduction by Hans Selye. New York: Hawthorn Books, Inc., 1961. Practical advice on the avoidance of cardiovascular disease resulting from stress, based principally on the technical monographs of Hans Selye.

Kollar, E. J. "Psychological Stress: A Re-evaluation." *J. Nerv. Men. Dis.* 132 (1961): 832–896. On the basis of the literature and personal observations, "the concept of stress has been extended to include inhibitory-conservatory shifts as well as excitatory shifts in homeostasis. These shifts may be either adaptive or maladaptive. If the response is prolonged in duration or inappropriate to the stress, pathophysiological and tissue changes may result."

Kositskiy, G. I., and Smirnov, V. S. *The Nervous System and "Stress."* Washington, D.C.: National Aeronautics and Space Administration, 1972. A well-documented technical monograph on the relationship between the role played by the nervous system (Pavlov) in resistance phenomena and hormonal reactions to stress (Selye). The nonhormonal aspects (including nervous mediation) of the G.A.S. are not considered. The extensive bibliography in this English translation will be a valuable source of references to the pertinent Soviet literature for those not speaking Russian. The original Russian edition was published by Nauka in 1970, under the same title.

Koster, M.; Musaph, H.; and Visser, P., eds. *Psychosomatics in Essential Hypertension*. Bibliotheca Psychiatrica et Neurologica, no. 144. Basel, Munich, New York: S. Karger, 1970. International symposium organized by the Dutch Society for Psychosomatic Research in 1968. Such topics as the methodology of blood pressure measurements, the role of emotional stress, and various psychosomatic aspects of disease have been covered in eight presentations, each followed by a discussion.

Kraus, H. *Backache, Stress and Tension: Their Cause, Prevention and Treatment*. New York: Simon & Schuster, Inc., 1965. Illustrated popular book on the role of stress in causing backache, with advice concerning physical therapy, mainly exercise, to combat this complication.

Kryter, K. D. *The Effects of Noise on Man*. New York, London: Academic Press, Inc., 1970. Detailed technical monograph on the effects of noise upon the ears and the body as a whole, with a comparatively short section on "Stress and Health" (914 refs.).

Laborit, H. *Organic Reaction to Stress and Shock* [Réaction organique à l'agression et choc].

Preface by R. Leriche. Paris: Masson & Cie. Editeurs, 1952. General review on the relationships between the concepts of various homeostatic mechanisms of Claude Bernard, Walter Cannon, and J. Reilly. Detailed description of functional and structural changes in the nervous, hormonal, and reticuloendothelial systems. In French.

——. *Stress and Cellular Function.* Philadelphia, Montreal: J. B. Lippincott Co., 1959. Cellular and biochemical aspects of stress phenomena, especially in relation to artificial hibernation and resuscitation.

Laszlo, E. *Introduction to Systems Philosophy— Toward a New Paradigm of Contemporary Thought.* Foreword by Ludwig von Bertalanffy. New York, Evanston, Ill., San Francisco, London: Harper Torchbooks, 1973. An excellent survey of systems philosophy as applied to artificial and natural systems. Special attention is given to "system-cybernetics," adaptive self-stabilization, adaptive self-organization and intra- and inter-systemic hierarchies. The endocrine feedback in biological rhythms is used as an example of adaptability in relation to homeostasis and the G.A.S. The bibliography contains an extensive list of the most important key references.

Lazarus, R. S. *Psychological Stress and the Coping*

*Process.* New York, Toronto, London: McGraw-Hill Book Co., 1966. Detailed and very competent discussion of stress in relation to psychology, with special reference to the problem of coping with threatening situations. Correlations between the adaptive mechanism of the central nervous system and the G.A.S. are given adequate attention throughout this volume.

Leithead, C. S., and Lind, A. R. *Heat Stress and Heat Disorders.* London: Cassell & Co., Ltd., 1964. Review of the literature and personal observations on the assessment, management, and control of heat stress and the diseases that may result from exposure to high temperatures.

Levi, L. *Stress: Sources, Management, and Prevention.* Foreword by Hans Selye. New York: Liveright Publishing Corporation, 1967. Very readable volume on the sources, management, and prevention of stress, emphasizing both the purely medical and psychological aspects of everyday experiences.

——, ed. *Emotional Stress.* Stockholm: *Försvars-medicin* 3, suppl. 2, 1967. International symposium arranged by the Swedish Delegation for Applied Medical Defense Research. A large number of speakers presented papers on the relationship between the G.A.S. and various psychological and biochemical (particularly hormonal) responses to emotional stressors of different kinds, especially those encountered in the army, navy, and air force.

——, ed. *Society, Stress and Disease.* New York, Toronto, London: Oxford University Press, 1971. International interdisciplinary symposium sponsored by the University of Uppsala and the WHO. The principal subjects for discussion were: definition of problems and objectives of stress research, relationships between the G.A.S. and social adjustment, neuroendocrine function, potentially pathogenic psychosocial stressors in today's society, epidemiological evidence for diseases produced by stressors, and possible ways of modifying or preventing psychosomatic diseases through social action. First formulation of the definition: "Biologic stress is the nonspecific response of the body to any demand made upon it." An excellent overview of contemporary ideas on the different somatic and psychic manifestations of stress. Rich source of useful references.

——, ed. *Stress and Distress in Response to Psychosocial Stimuli.* Foreword by Hans Selye. Oxford, New York, Toronto, Sydney, Brunswick: Pergamon Press, 1972. Very thoughtful analysis of the literature and of the author's personal observations on the G.A.S. in relation to psychosocial stimuli. Detailed description of the methodology, including hormone determinations. Special emphasis is placed upon pleasant and unpleasant psychosocial stimuli, stress reactions to sexual stimulation, and the relationship between psychological and physiological reactions during acute and chronic exposure to stressors in man.

Levine, S. "Stress and Behavior." *Sci. Amer.* 224 (1971):26–31. Very readable popularized review on the role of pituitary and adrenal hormones in the regulation of behavior during the G.A.S. "It may be that effective behavior depends upon some optimum level of stress."

Lewinsohn, P. M. "Some Individual Differences in Physiological Reactivity to Stress." *J. Comp. Physiol. Psychol.* 49 (1956):271–277. Technical paper on physiological reactivity to stress in patients with duodenal ulcer, essential hypertension, and neuromuscular tension. Modified Cold Pressor Test and Failure Test were used.

Liebman, S., ed. *Stress Situations.* Philadelphia, Montreal: J. B. Lippincott Co., 1955. Anthology of publications on emotional reactions to the stress of frustration, illness, catastrophes, marriage, fertility and sterility, divorce, death, and suicide presented in highly simplified lay language.

Margetts, E. L. "Historical Notes on Psychosomatic Medicine." In *Recent Developments in Psychosomatic Medicine*, edited by E. D. Wittkower and R. A. Cleghorn, pp. 41–68. London: Pitman Medical Pub. Co., Ltd., 1954. Motto of C. H. Parry (1755–1822): "It is much more important to know what sort of a patient has a disease, than what sort of a disease a patient has." The history of ideas about correlations between man, body, and cell is traced back to antiquity and followed through up to the publication in 1950 of Selye's first detailed monograph on stress.

Marxer, W. L., and Cowgill, G. R., eds. *The Art of Predictive Medicine: The Early Detection of Deteriorative Trends (Proceedings of a Symposium)*. Springfield, Ill.: Charles C. Thomas, Publisher, 1967. An anthology of various publications on the early detection and prevention of degenerative diseases, with a special section on stress.

Maslow, A. H. *Motivation and Personality*. New York: Harper & Brothers, 1954. Perceptive analysis of motivation in general by an author trained in Gestalt psychology, psychoanalysis, and anthropology. Relationships to physiology and stress reactions in particular are not dealt with.

Mason, J. W. "A Re-evaluation of the Concept of

'Nonspecificity' in Stress Theory." *J. Psychiat. Res.* 8 (1971): 323–333. Brief but excellent analysis of the evidence contradicting Selye's definition of stress. Mason states that stress "may simply be the psychological apparatus involved in emotional or arousal reactions to threatening or unpleasant factors in the life situation as a whole." However, in a letter (which he has allowed me to quote) Mason clarifies the preceding sentence by saying that "when psychological influences are minimized, such stressors as heat and fasting do not provoke certain hormonal responses characteristic of stress, although other stressors such as cold and hypoxia continue to evoke these hormonal responses."

McKenna, M. *Revitalize Yourself! The Techniques of Staying Youthful.* Foreword by J. A. Bailey. New York: Hawthorn Books, Inc., 1972. Monograph containing practical advice, in popular terms, on how to stay fit. A special section deals with "Stress and Its Aging Effects" in the light of the G.A.S., and throughout the well-illustrated text frequent attention is called to the beneficial effects of the revitalizing stressors, especially exercises.

McLuhan, M. *Understanding Media.* New York, Toronto, London: McGraw-Hill Book Co., 1964. Monograph on the author's much-discussed and rather unique philosophy, with many references to the possible implications of the stress theory in human behavior.

"Medical Aspects of Torture." *The Lancet*, 20 October 1973, pp. 900–901. Brief report of a medical group under the auspices of Amnesty International which met in London to consider medical aspects of methods of coercion by torture, involving the infliction of extreme physical and mental pain resulting in severe stress. A brief list of pertinent publications is attached.

Menninger, K. "Regulatory Devices of the Ego Under Major Stress." *Int. J. Psychoanal.* 35 (1962):412–420. Psychoanalytical study of the stress syndrome as a mental homeostatic reaction. It is concluded that "in its effort to control dangerous impulses under such circumstances and thereby prevent or retard the disintegrative process which threatens, the ego initiates emergency regulatory devices which fall into five hierarchically arranged and specifically characterized groups, representing increasingly greater degrees of failure in integration."

——; Mayman, M.; and Pruyser, P. *The Vital Balance: The Life Process in Mental Health and Illness.* New York: The Viking Press, Inc., 1963. Well-documented treatise with an extensive bibliography on psychosomatic medicine. Special emphasis is placed upon coping devices in everyday life, aggression, neurotic behavior, and the importance of a personal relationship between physician and patient.

Mitchell, H. H., and Edman, M. *Nutrition and Climatic Stress*. Springfield, Ill.: Charles C. Thomas, Publisher, 1951. Technical discussion of observations on stress caused by cold, heat, high altitude, and acceleration in relation to the nutrition of man (more than 750 refs.).

Moss, G. E. *Illness, Immunity, and Social Interaction: The Dynamics of Biosocial Resonation*. New York, London, Sydney, Toronto: John Wiley & Sons, Inc., 1973. Effect of social interactions upon the development of illness and immunity.

Müller, K. E. *Introduction to General Psychology* [Einführung in die Allgemeine Psychologie]. Stuttgart: Ferdinand Enke Verlag, 1965. Textbook on psychology with a penetrating analysis of psychosomatic interrelations, especially with regard to the stress syndrome. In German.

Musaph, H., and Mettrop, P. J. G., eds. "The Role of Aggression in Human Pathology (Symposium organized at the 5th World Congress for Psychiatry, Mexico City, 1971)." *Psychother. Psychosom.* 20 (1972):241–320. Proceedings of an international symposium on psychosomatic aspects of illness with special reference to the role of aggressive behavior and several discussions concerning the participation of the G.A.S.

Orr, W. H. *Hormones, Health and Happiness*. New York: The Macmillan Co., 1954. Popular description of the role of endocrine glands in disease, with a special chapter on the alarm reaction.

Page, R. C. *How to Lick Executive Stress*. New York: Simon & Schuster; An Essandess Special Edition, 1966. A medical consultant to various governmental and industrial management groups and former Chairman of the Board of the Occupational Health Institute gives advice in simple language on how to apply the stress theory to problems of executives in overcoming the constant pressures of their occupations. No reference is made to technical literature.

Pence, R. J.; Chambers, R. D.; and Viray, M. S. " 'Psychogenetic Stress' and Autointoxication in the Honey Bee." *Nature* 200 (1963):930–932. Discussion of the G.A.S. as it applies to a social insect such as the honey bee.

Pfeiffer, C. J., ed. *Peptic Ulcer*. Philadelphia, Toronto: J. B. Lippincott Co., 1971. Collection of highly technical papers on the experimental production and treatment of peptic ulcers in the stomach and duodenum. Special emphasis is placed by many of the authors upon the role of stress (several hundred refs.).

Raab, W., ed. *Prevention of Ischemic Heart Disease*. Springfield, Ill.: Charles C. Thomas, Publisher, 1966. "First International Congress on Preventive Cardiology," composed of highly technical reports by numerous outstanding cardiologists. Several sections deal particularly with the effects of stress.

Romano, J., ed. *Adaptation*. Ithaca, N.Y.: Cornell University Press, 1949. Anthology of papers on adaptation to various environmental factors, with main emphasis upon emotional, intellectual, and neurotic reactions. The G.A.S. is not mentioned.

Scharrer, E., and Scharrer, B. *Neuroendocrinology*. New York, London: Columbia University Press, 1963. Highly technical treatise on the relationships between endocrine glands and the nervous system. A separate chapter is devoted to the stress concept based on the works of Cannon and Selye. An extensive bibliography gives easy access to the relevant technical literature.

Schindler, J. A. *How to Live 365 Days a Year*. Englewood Cliffs, N.J.: Prentice-Hall, Inc., 1959. Recommendations on how to avoid psychosomatic illness, based primarily on the stress concept. Written exclusively for the lay reader.

Scott, J. P. *Aggression.* Chicago: University of Chicago Press, 1958. Popularized description of the factors regulating aggressive behavior, with only cursory reference to the G.A.S.

Sorenson, S. *The Quest of Wholeness.* Reykjavik: Prentsmidja Jons Helgasonar, 1971. An evaluation of the yoga discipline from the point of view of neurophysiology, with special reference to the stress syndrome.

Sos, J., Gáti, T.: Csalay, L.; and Dési, I. *Pathology of Civilization Diseases.* Budapest: Akadémiai Kiadó, 1971. Many maladies largely due to stress are considered to be "diseases of civilization." A special section is devoted to the role of corticoids and stress in the development of peptic ulcers.

Still, H. *In Quest of Quiet.* Harrisburg, Pa.: Stackpole Books, 1970. Popular description of the harm which can be inflicted by noise of the city, high-speed aircraft, and industry. Mainly based on the author's empirical observations and many impressive quotations from the daily press. Strictly scientific publications are only occasionally cited.

Stremple, J. F.; Mori, H.; Lev, R.; and Jerzy Glass, G. B. "The Stress Ulcer Syndrome" *Curr.*

*Probl. Surg.*, April 1973, pp. 1–64. Monograph on the causation and therapy of stress ulcers, with many personal observations gathered during the Vietnam war. An instructive, historical introduction mentions reports of gastrointestinal ulcers following combat wounds, burns, and infections from the early Roman wars throughout the literature of the 18th and 19th century up to the present time (281 refs.).

*Symposium on Stress.* Washington, D.C.: Army Medical Service Graduate School, 1958. A conference on stress sponsored by the Division of Medical Sciences National Research Council and the Army Medical Service Graduate School, Walter Reed Army Medical Center, Washington, D. C. Numerous papers on the hormonal and nervous regulation of stress responses, with special reference to combat situations, interpersonal relationships, nutrition, and adaptation to catastrophic events.

Szép, I. *The Importance of Stress in Animal Husbandry*. [A stress jelentósége az állattenyésztésben]. Budapest: Agroinform, 1968. The importance of stress in veterinary medicine with an extensive literature survey on relevant observations concerning the G.A.S. In Hungarian.

Tanner, J. M., ed. *Stress and Psychiatric Disorder*. Oxford: Basil Blackwell & Mott, Ltd., 1960.

Second Oxford Conference of the Mental Health Research Fund, with contributions from many specialists in the psychological and somatic aspects of the stress concept. The main subjects are: disorganization of behavior during stress in man and animals; physiological responses to stressors; prevention and treatment of psychiatric stress reactions.

Terigi, A. T. *Longevity and Vitality* [Longevità e Vitalità]. Bologna: Casa Editrice Prof. Riccardo Patron, 1967. A monograph on the traumatic and psychic problems of senility with special reference to the G.A.S. In Italian.

Thiessen, D. D. "Population Density and Behavior: A Review of Theoretical and Physiological Contributions." *Tex. Rep. Biol. Med.* 22 (1964): 266–314. Survey of the technical literature on crowding which can cause distress and thereby limit overpopulation (about 225 refs.).

Timiras, P. S. *Developmental Physiology and Aging.* New York: The Macmillan Co., 1972. A textbook on aging with a chapter on "Decline in Homeostatic Regulation" having special reference to the G.A.S.

Toffler, A. *Future Shock.* New York: Random House, Inc., 1970. A very readable popular book about the stressor effect of the continuous changes in modern society and the way in which we adapt—or fail to adapt—to the future (359 refs.).

Visotsky, H. M.; Hamburg, D. A.; Goss, M. E.; and Lebovits, B. Z. "Coping Behavior Under Extreme Stress." *Arch. Gen. Psychiat.* 5 (1961):423–448. Observations on adaptive behavior (or its failure) in patients with severe poliomyelitis.

Warmbrand, M. *Add Years to Your Heart.* New York: Whittier Books, Inc., 1956. Highly simplified set of practical recommendations for cardiac patients, with a special section on lessons derived from work on the G.A.S.

Weiner, H., ed. *Duodenal Ulcer.* Advances in Psychosomatic Medicine, vol. 6. Basel: S. Karger, 1971. Collection of Nine publications (each followed by a discussion) mainly on the role of psychological factors in the development of duodenal ulcers in man. Animal experiments and basic research on pathogenesis are also considered.

Weiss, E., and English, O. S. *Psychosomatic Medicine.* Philadelphia, London: W. B. Saunders Co., 1949. Extensive, though by now somewhat outdated, textbook of psychosomatic medicine with a rich collection of historically interesting references.

Welch, B. L., and Welch, A. S., eds. *Physiological Effects of Noise.* New York, London: Plenum

Press, Inc., 1970. Extensive text on the pathogenic effect of noise upon animals and man, with numerous references concerning the stressor action of sound which can cause "diseases of adaptation." Rich source of pertinent literature.

Wiggers, C. J. *Physiology of Shock*. London: Oxford University Press, 1950. Technical treatise on shock, with a few pages on its relationship to the alarm reaction.

Wolff, H. G. *Stress and Disease*. Springfield, Ill.: Charles C. Thomas, Publisher, 1953. Brief résumé in semitechnical language on the relationship between stress and disease (210 refs).

———. *Stress and Disease*. 2d ed., rev. Edited by Wolf and H. Goodell. Springfield, Ill.: Charles C. Thomas, Publisher, 1968. In this expanded and updated edition, emphasis is placed on protective adaptive reactions which can play a decisive role in the resistance of man to the common stressors of modern life. Special sections are devoted to "stress interviews" and the part played by stress in headache, migraine, and respiratory, cardiovascular, and digestive diseases in relation to social adjustment and a healthy philosophy of life.

Yates, F. E., and Maran, J. W. *Stimulation and Inhibition of Adrenocorticotropin (ACTH)*

*Release.* Handbook of Physiology, edited by W. Sawyer and E. Knobil. Washington, D.C.: American Physiological Society, forthcoming. Careful and well-illustrated review especially concerned with feedback mechanisms regulating ACTH release during stress (395 refs.).

Zatykó, J. "Is Selye's Stress Theory Applicable to Plants?" *Az élet és Tudomány Kalendáriuma* 73 (1973):37–41. Brief summary in lay language of scientific evidence indicating that stress can occur in plants. In Hungarian.

Zuckerman, M. "Perceptual Isolation as a Stress Situation." *Arch. gen. Psychiat.* 11 (1964): 255–276. Careful evaluation of the literature (68 refs.) on biochemical and physiological responses to isolation produced by various techniques in normal and abnormal individuals. "Sensory deprivation" (darkness and quiet) is compared with "perceptual deprivation" (unpatterned light and constant "white noise").

——; Albright, R. J.; Marks, C. S.; and Miller, G. L. "Stress and Hallucinatory Effects of Perceptual Isolation and Confinement." *Psychol. Monogr.* 76, no. 30 (1962):1–15. Observations on student nurses subjected to perceptual isolation through various techniques. The resulting loss of orientation, difficulties in directed thinking, anxiety from personal thoughts, and increasing somatic discomfort lead to a mounting stress reaction in most subjects. Hallucinations are also common.

# Index

# Index